The AACRAO 2003
Academic Record and Transcript Guide

AACRAO®
1910

American Association of Collegiate Registrars and Admissions Officers

Library of Congress Cataloging-in-Publication Data

American Association of Collegiate Registrars and Admissions Officers.
Task Force on the Academic Record and Transcript Guide 2003.

The AACRAO 2003 academic record and transcript guide/(prepared by
the Task Force on the Academic Record and Transcript Guide 2003 of the
American Association of Collegiate Registrars and Admissions Officers).

p. cm. — (AACRAO professional development & education series) Rev.
ed. of: AACRAO academic record and transcript guide/prepared by the
AACRAO Task Force on the Academic Record and Transcript Guide, Paul
Aucoin...[et al.] 1996. Includes bibliographical references and index.

ISBN 1-57858-045-5 (pbk. : alk. paper)

1. Universities and colleges—United States—Records
    and correspondence.
2. College registrars—United States.
3. Universities and colleges—United States—Admission.

I. AACRAO Task Force on the Academic Record and Transcript
    Guide. AACRAO academic record and transcript guide.
II. Title.
III. Series.

LB2341.A52 2003
651.5'04—dc21

2003004932

Prepared by:

The Task Force on *The 2003 Academic Record and Transcript Guide* of the
American Association of Collegiate Registrars and Admissions Officers

Chair

PATRICK MILLER
Registrar and Director of Enrollment Management
Texas Christian University (Fort Worth, TX)

Members

DR. PATRICIA COVINGTON
Associate Director of Admissions and Records
Southern Illinois University Carbondale (Carbondale, IL)

DR. BARBARA LAUREN
Associate Director, Research
American Association of Collegiate Registrars and
Admissions Officers (Washington, DC)

ROBERT MORLEY
Associate Registrar
University of Southern California
(Los Angeles, CA)

RICHARD SKEEL
Director of Academic Records
University of Oklahoma (Norman, OK)

JOHN T. STEWART
College Registrar
Miami-Dade Community College, Kendall Campus
(Miami, FL)

STUART TERRASS
Registrar
Mount Union College (Alliance, OH)

CHARLES TOOMAJIAN
Registrar and Associate Dean for Student Services
Williams College (Williamstown, MA)

TEYA WALKKER
Director, Student Advising
Fielding Graduate Institute (Santa Barbara, CA)

Contents

Acknowledgements

In one sense, work on the 2003 *Guide* started over a hundred years ago, when registrars first began to document and share the fruits of their labor. Previous versions of *The Academic Record and Transcript Guide* have relied heavily on the practice and wisdom of our predecessors. This current version is no exception. The debt is large.

In addition, we have asked our colleagues for information and opinions: in formal surveys, in discussion sessions at conferences, and informally as we gather. This input has been invaluable and has framed many of the discussions necessary to generate the *Guide*.

The nine members of the Task Force, representing more years of experience than any would care to admit, have unselfishly contributed wisdom, insight, time, and effort. Their diversity and commitment to the profession have produced a guide that will serve equally well the many types of institutions represented among AACRAO members.

Finally, the *Guide* could not have been prepared without AACRAO staff member Barbara Lauren. Barbara served as muse for this project. In the end, when everyone had contributed chapters, Barbara took on the huge task of molding diverse work elements into a complete whole while allowing the Task Force to maintain ownership. The whole which Barbara created is certainly much greater than the sum of its parts.

Patrick Miller
Task Force Chair

Introduction

❶ ② ③ ④ ⑤ ⑥ ⑦ ⑧ ⑨ ⑩ ⑪ ⑫

Registrars have always been guardians of the integrity of an institution's records and degrees. In recent years, and particularly since 1996, the date of AACRAO's most recent previous *Guide*, registrars and records professionals have increasingly faced the need to reconcile two competing demands: the need to provide accurate information promptly to various constituencies, and the need to safeguard privacy.

In addition, the advent of new student information systems has complicated both of those considerations: it is now easier both to disseminate information promptly upon authorized request—even if the format is often determined by the system chosen!—and, deliberately or through inadvertence, to disseminate information to unauthorized parties.

In this edition of *The AACRAO 2003 Academic Record and Transcript Guide*, we have tried to combine the best of the old—such as a thorough discussion of Database and Transcript Components—with practical guidance for new or evolving situations.

Among such situations are three current issues that have been the subject of widespread discussion in the profession: Notation on the transcript of academic or disciplinary ineligibility to re-enroll; use of Social Security Numbers; and documentation of name changes.

In order to facilitate easy use of this *Guide*, we here present a brief overview of each chapter.

In the following chapter—Chapter Two—we discuss the terms "database," "academic record," and "transcript," and make some distinctions based on the historical evolution of those concepts. In essence, we emphasize the distinction between the full database and the transcript. Especially with the advent of computer technology, the full database can now contain many items which are either optional, or not recommended, to be included on the transcript.

In Chapter Three, "Database and Transcript Components," we present 49 data elements, and make recommendations as to whether their use is Essential, Recommended, Optional, or Not Recommended—regarding both the database and the transcript. Note that in Appendix B, we present a "Self-Audit" exercise concerning what should, and should not be, included on transcripts.

In Chapter Four, we present a concise guide to the "Key to the Transcript." We list 19 items that are essential to be included in the key, and nine optional items.

Chapter Five addresses "Some Current Issues" in three sections:

■ Recording Academic and Disciplinary Actions on Transcripts;
■ Use of Social Security Numbers: In the Student Database; on the Academic Transcript; as a Student ID; and for Financial Aid Programs; and
■ Name Change Recommendation.

NOTE In Appendix A, we also present and explain the highlights of the two surveys that AACRAO conducted in the spring of 2002, concerning institutional practice as to each of the above items (Appendix A, Survey A) and registrars' views as to what they considered to be best practice for an institution of their type (Appendix A, Survey B).

Chapter Six updates the section formerly called "Release of Academic Record Information." It is now entitled "FERPA, USA PATRIOT ACT, and Their Impact on Release of Student Education Records." It briefly discusses FERPA; refers the reader to *The AACRAO 2001 FERPA Guide*; and succinctly discusses the PATRIOT Act. Since FERPA and the PATRIOT ACT are inevitably subject to change, we refer users of this *Guide* to the AACRAO Web site, specifically its Compliance page, for timely ongoing updates. In addition, the FERPA chapter contains its own bibliography section, called

"Additional Resources," which includes websites from AACRAO and elsewhere, as well as references to hard-copy material.

Chapter Seven updates the discussion of "Transcript Services: Issuing, Withholding, and Faxing." In the section on "issuing transcripts," there is a new sub-section on how to proceed when your institution is the custodian of record for an institution that has closed.

Chapter Eight is a succinct summary of "Fraudulent Transcripts"—what to look for, both good and bad. Note that in Appendix D, we present a one-page set of "Guidelines for Fighting Fraud."

Chapter Nine is an expanded and updated discussion of "Transcription of Nontraditional Learning" (formerly "The Transcript in the Changing Educational Environment"). It draws a distinction between identifying the origin of the coursework (recommended) and identifying the mode of delivery (not recommended). It discusses the transcription of nine types of nontraditional learning: Experiential Learning; Credit by Examination; Distance Learning; Independent Study; Study Abroad; Military Education; Corporate Education; External Degree Programs; and Continuing Education. Note that in Appendix C, we present "Examples of Nontraditional Transcript Entries," and in Appendix E, we present a "Sample Transcript and Key."

Chapter Ten updates the discussion of Continuing Education Unit (CEU) Records, and references the websites of both the American Council on Education (its Center for Adult Learning) and the International Association for Continuing Education and Training.

Chapter Eleven, the "Security of Records" section, updates the discussion of physical security and also electronic data storage, security training for staff, and additional safeguards and challenges.

Chapter Twelve clarifies the two standards—one current (EDI) and one emerging (XML)—for "Electronic Standards for Data Interchange."

We also include six Appendices. In addition to the five that have already been mentioned, we conclude with Appendix F, which describes the "Evolution of the AACRAO Academic Record and Transcript Guide." AACRAO first addressed the subject one year after its founding in 1910.

Finally, we also include an expanded and updated Glossary; an expanded, updated, and annotated list of "Additional Resources," which points the records professional to further sources of information; and an Index.

We hope that this work will be of immediate and continuing use to registrars and information professionals at all stages of their careers, and in a variety of settings.

Chapter Two

Database, Academic Record, and Transcript:
Distinctions Based on Historical Perspective

① ❷ ③ ④ ⑤ ⑥ ⑦ ⑧ ⑨ ⑩ ⑪ ⑫

Historical Perspective

The office and functions of the registrar date back to the great medieval universities of Bologna, Paris, and Oxford (Quann, 1979). As early as the twelfth century, the beadle was an official who proclaimed announcements, exacted fines, and helped the academic operation run smoothly.

The first academic officer with the title of "registrar" was appointed in 1446 at Oxford (Quann, 1979). That officer's duties were "to give form and permanence to the university's public acts, to draft its letters, to make copies of its documents, and to register the names of its graduates and their "examinatory sermons" (Mallet, 1924).

In the United States, at the first institution of higher education (Harvard College, established in 1636), the registrar's academic record-keeping function was initially a part-time duty assigned to a faculty member. The position rapidly became professionalized, however, as student enrollment in colleges grew. Along with the college president, the treasurer, and the librarian, the registrar was among the first administrative officers to become a specialist (Quann, 1979). Among institutions belonging to the Association of American Universities, fewer than 10 percent had registrars as of 1880, but 25 percent had designated them by 1890, as had 42 percent by 1900, and 76 percent by 1910—the founding year of the American Association of Collegiate Registrars (AACR), now the American Association of Collegiate Registrars and Admissions Officers (AACRAO) (Quann, 1979). (AACRAO added "and Admissions Officers" in 1949.)

The office of the registrar exists to serve the needs of students, to respond to requests of the faculty and administration for data, and to safeguard the integrity of the institution's records and degrees.

Evolution of the Transcript Out of the Academic Record

In the nineteenth century, a college or university "student information system" consisted of two ledger books. One was a compilation of class rosters, with final examination and course grades posted by each name. The other was the "matriculants' book," with demographic information about each student: often, the home county, the parents' names, and the student's religious denomination.

Since all students followed the same curriculum, transcripts were not needed, and few were prepared. The registrar simply noted the degree received or, if the student did not graduate, the number of years of study completed. Such certifications were usually prepared as letters, in response to a request for information.

About the turn of the century, spurred by the new elective system of course offerings and by the introduction of major and minor fields of study, colleges and universities began to shift the focus from the graduating cohort, to the individual student. Records now consisted of a separate page for each student—a page which combined demographic information with a compilation of the student's individualized set of courses. All the pertinent information about any one student was contained on one ledger page.

In the early years of the twentieth century, the ledger page became a record card—a document that contained essentially the same information as the ledger page, but could be more easily handled and filed. This document became known as the Permanent Record Card. The Permanent Record Card was the major database of its day—a repository of much miscellaneous information related to the student.

The transcript is that extract of the student's record which reflects his or her academic performance at the institution. After World War II, with the increase in student enrollment, registrars often photocopied the Permanent Record Card to serve as a transcript. Photocopying the permanent record card, much faster and cheaper than typing an extract of the record, meant that the transcript was then synonymous with the full database for that student. Many such records even showed where other transcripts had been sent!

Even in an era when privacy requirements were not yet enshrined in the law, this was obviously not an optimum system. Now, with the advent of computer technology, the content of documents and reports can be customized according to the needs (and the right to know) of the recipient.

Most important of all is the need to remember the distinction between the full database and the transcript. The full database can contain many items that are either optional, or not recommended, to be included on the transcript.

In our setting forth of "Database and Transcript Components," we make use of four categories of information:
- Essential;
- Recommended;
- Optional; and
- Not Recommended.

In many instances—date of birth, for example—the full information may be essential to the database but merely recommended (and even then, with month and day only) for the transcript.

We hope that the following list of data elements will be helpful to records and registration officers in maintaining the distinction between information that is appropriate to be maintained in the database, and the smaller subset of information that is appropriate to be placed on an official transcript.

It is the responsibility of the issuing institution to be certain that the document transmitted as a transcript is appropriate for the use intended, that it contains at the least the essential data elements specified in this publication, and that it is consistent with the legal guidelines under which the institution operates.

Chapter Three

Database and Transcript Components

①②❸④⑤⑥⑦⑧⑨⑩⑪⑫

Before the advent of ready access to computerization, the transcript contained many data elements no longer necessary or appropriate for the transcript, simply because a transcript was a convenient repository for data. Now, the database is the chief repository of student-related information. Indeed, the database includes many items which should not be included in a transcript, because transcripts are disseminated to third parties. The database also contains other elements that should be included only in a different format or level of completeness from that shown on transcripts.

Identification of the Institution

Name, Institution

In multi-part institutions, the institutional name should be the degree-granting entity. The transcript key should include previous names of the institution, at least for a period of transition (5 years), and should identify the new and the old name(s).

DATABASE   Essential
TRANSCRIPT   Essential

Location (City, State, Zip Code, Telephone Number, Website)

May be a part of the transcript key.

DATABASE   Essential
TRANSCRIPT   Essential

Identifying Code

It is helpful to the recipient of the transcript if one or more of the following identifying codes is noted on the transcript: ACT, CEEB, or FICE code. When reported, the source of the code should be identified.

DATABASE   Recommended
TRANSCRIPT   Recommended

Identification of the Student

Name

The name should be the documented legal name of the student. (See Chapter Five, discussing recommendation as to documentation for name change.) Databases usually include all variant forms of a student's name, including previous surnames and nicknames or names called by, but only the current name is absolutely necessary on the transcript.

DATABASE   Essential
TRANSCRIPT   Essential

NAME CHANGE RECOMMENDATION

Entry of the Name—Keep all names of the student in a sequence in the database. If you use only one name, use the name of current attendance. Otherwise, if your data entry system allows, and your institution wishes, you can carry both with the most current name at date of enrollment (specify which).

Documentation Needed for Name Change—Certified copy of a marriage license, court order, or dissolution decree reflecting the new name in full. For non-US citizens: Current passport or official proof of identity, certified by US embassy abroad or by the appropriate foreign embassy in the US.

Maintenance of the Name—May have multiple entry points, but responsibility for monitoring integrity of the name rests with the academic records department.

Name Changes (current students)—If your system allows, carry both old and new names. Otherwise, use the current name.

Name Changes (former students)—If your system allows, carry both old and new names. Be certain to change the name on the transcript if presented with a marriage license, court order showing change of name, or divorce decree mandating restoration of birth name. Otherwise, recommended. Changing of the diploma is not recommended.

Identification Number

We recommend that institutions create their own student ID numbers as the primary student identifier in the database. Regulations implementing the Internal Revenue Code require institutions of higher education to collect the SSN for students on whose behalf tuition is paid. Hence, we recommend the use of the SSN as a secondary identifier in the database. See further discussion in Chapter Five.

`DATABASE` Recommended—Institution-created student ID as the primary student identifier in the database. Essential—SSN as secondary cross-check.
`TRANSCRIPT` Recommended—SSN

Address

The address is not an appropriate part of the transcript. Nonetheless, various addresses—including local, billing, emergency, permanent, grade-mailing, and e-mail—are needed in the database. The e-mail appearing in the database should be the institution's officially assigned e-mail, with a student option to receive e-mail at another e-mail address.

`DATABASE` Essential
`TRANSCRIPT` Not Recommended

Date of birth

The appearance of the date of birth on the transcript has increasingly become a source of concern to many who perceive it as a basis for age discrimination. Although this data item is essential to a good database, only the month and day should be included on the transcript, omitting the year of birth.

`DATABASE` Essential
`TRANSCRIPT` Recommended (month/day only)

Place of birth

May be a source of perceived discrimination. Sometimes useful in establishing residency for fee purposes. It is essential to collect this information for international students applying for an F-I student visa.

`DATABASE` Optional
`TRANSCRIPT` Not Recommended

Gender

Necessary for IPEDS reporting requirements. As to the transcript, not recommended.

`NOTE` While collection of this data element is necessary for IPEDS reporting, institutions should exercise caution in placing such a question on their application forms. Institutions may ask for, but may not require, information as to this data element on their applications.

`DATABASE` Essential (but see commentary above)
`TRANSCRIPT` Not Recommended

Race and Ethnicity

Necessary for IPEDS reporting requirements.

`NOTE` While collection of this data element is necessary for IPEDS reporting, institutions should exercise caution in placing such a question on their application forms. Institutions may ask for, but may not require, information as to this data element on their applications.

`DATABASE` Essential (but see commentary above)
`TRANSCRIPT` Not Recommended (unless required by law)

Marital Status

Usually not pertinent, unless the institution offers benefits to married students or their families; then database only.

DATABASE Optional
TRANSCRIPT Not Recommended

Religious Preference

Sometimes useful to campus activities, especially in church-related institutions, but should not be reported on the transcript. May be construed as an invasion of privacy.

DATABASE Optional
TRANSCRIPT Not Recommended

Disability

Disability information should be maintained in the database, but only if reported by the student. Never include disability on the transcript.

NOTE The same cautions expressed as to gender and race/ethnicity apply also to disability.

DATABASE Essential (if reported by the student)
TRANSCRIPT Not Recommended

Citizenship and/or INS Status for F or M Visa Holders and Students Applying for Federal Financial Aid

As to F or M ("student") visa holders: The INS requires institutions to maintain and report up-to-date data through the SEVIS system.

For students applying for Federal student financial aid, there is a data-match with the INS.

DATABASE Essential
TRANSCRIPT Not Recommended

Basis for Admission

Secondary School Graduation or Equivalent

Note: Secondary school information may not be relevant to graduate or professional schools.

[13]

NAME, LOCATION OF SCHOOL
Both name and location are needed to distinguish between schools with similar names

DATABASE Essential
TRANSCRIPT Not Recommended

SCHOOL CODE
CEEB or ACT code identifying schools

DATABASE Optional
TRANSCRIPT Not Recommended

DATE OF GRADUATION
May be perceived as a basis for age discrimination.

DATABASE Essential
TRANSCRIPT Not Recommended

Test Scores

NATIONAL TEST SCORES
Usually ACT or SAT.

DATABASE Essential
TRANSCRIPT Not Recommended

STATE-MANDATED
Example is TASS in Texas.

DATABASE Essential
TRANSCRIPT Not Recommended (unless required by state law)

College Credits Earned in High School

Some states mandate that state institutions accept such credits. Essential in both database and transcript if your school accepts such credits.

DATABASE Essential
TRANSCRIPT Essential

Previous Colleges or Universities Attended

Institutions may choose to post this information only from institutions from which credit has been transferred. However, the history of the previous institutions attended may be helpful to the receiving institution, regardless of credit awarded. Professional schools may choose to omit this information when it is unrelated to the professional program

DATABASE Essential
TRANSCRIPT Essential

NAME AND LOCATION OF INSTITUTION
DATABASE Essential
TRANSCRIPT Essential

PERIOD OF ATTENDANCE
DATABASE Essential
TRANSCRIPT Recommended

DEGREE RECEIVED
DATABASE Essential
TRANSCRIPT Recommended

YEAR DEGREE CONFERRED
DATABASE Essential
TRANSCRIPT Recommended

SCHOOL CODE
DATABASE Recommended
TRANSCRIPT Optional

CONCURRENT HS AND COLLEGE ATTENDANCE
DATABASE Essential
TRANSCRIPT Essential

Record of Work Pursued

Terms of Attendance

The trend is to include precise dates of the beginning and end of the term. Calendars should be described in detail in the transcript key or the course identification.

DATABASE Essential
TRANSCRIPT Essential

Withdrawal Date

Used for full withdrawal from the institution prior to the end of the term.

DATABASE Essential
TRANSCRIPT Recommended

Course Identification

Includes department or discipline identifier, course number, course title, and special information, such as taught as an honors course.

Note: In the database it is essential to maintain a historical cross-reference of changed course numbers for the same course.

Also: Maintain a listing of department abbreviations.

DATABASE Essential
TRANSCRIPT Essential

Amount of Credit

The amount of credit the course carries

| DATABASE | Essential |
| TRANSCRIPT | Essential |

Unit of Credit

Credit may be quarter, semester, or some different base. This information should be included in the transcript key.

| DATABASE | Essential |
| TRANSCRIPT | Essential |

Grades

The grade earned in each course, whether used in averages or not, must be shown on the transcript. Any exception must be included in the key.

| DATABASE | Essential |
| TRANSCRIPT | Essential |

Term GPA

Grade Point Averages are computed by varying methods, especially with reference to repeated courses. May be dynamically computed. The practice of showing GPAs for each session is much less common than that of showing the cumulative average. Historically, the practice of showing a cumulative average for each term has been used mainly by those institutions which photocopy hard copy permanent record cards as transcripts.

Note: If an A+ results in a GPA greater than the range indicated in the key, then that fact should be included in the key, as well. See also next entry.

| DATABASE | Essential |
| TRANSCRIPT | Recommended |

Cumulative GPA

Although the cumulative GPA traditionally has been reflected on most transcripts, it is not an essential item for inclusion there. In truth, most receiving bodies, especially other institutions, recompute the GPA according to their own rules, without regard to that reflected on the transcript. If the GPA, whether cumulative or by session, is reflected on the transcript, then it is recommended that the key contain information on how the average is computed (how repeated courses are computed; what, if any, courses are omitted from the comparison; etc.).

[15]

| DATABASE | Essential |
| TRANSCRIPT | Optional |

Term Grade Points

Grade point earned each term.

| DATABASE | Essential |
| TRANSCRIPT | Recommended |

Cumulative Credits, Grade Points, GPA

Refer to descriptions of "Grades," "Term GPA," "Cumulative GPA," and "Term Grade Points," above.

| DATABASE | Essential |
| TRANSCRIPT | Essential (if grades are not recorded in letter or number form) |

Narrative Evaluation

Used by some institutions in lieu of traditional letter grades.

| DATABASE | Essential |
| TRANSCRIPT | Essential (if grades are not recorded in letter or number form) |

Demonstrated Competencies

Nonclassroom experiences for which credit is awarded.

NOTE Demonstrated competencies imply the awarding of credit; they should not be confused with demonstrated proficiencies (see Glossary).

DATABASE Recommended
TRANSCRIPT Recommended

Transfer Credits Accepted

COURSES, GRADES, CREDIT PER COURSE

This is an essential part of the database for degree audit and for academic advising. Coursework should be shown with dates of work taken. As for inclusion on the transcript, many institutions list the actual coursework, which is helpful to the receiving institution(s). However, it is not essential to do so, unless the state requires it.

NOTE If courses from another institution are posted to a transcript, those credits should not be transferred without receipt of the original transcript.

NOTE In some states, the state authority requires that state institutions accept all credits awarded by in-state institutions—but many of those credits will not apply to the student's major or minor. So, the number of credits on the transcript may not tell you which courses count toward the major or concentration, but only the total amount of credit accepted.

DATABASE Essential
TRANSCRIPT Optional

CREDIT SUMMARY

Essential part of database; may be computed dynamically. Credit hours accepted should be shown on the transcript, as should dates of attendance.

DATABASE Essential
TRANSCRIPT Recommended

Academic Status

Good Standing

Only academic statuses which interrupt a student's continued enrollment should be reflected on the transcript.

DATABASE Essential
TRANSCRIPT Not Recommended

Academic Probation

Needed in database to make possible the application of academic rules or standards. Unless probation interrupts a student's continued enrollment, it should not appear on the transcript. Changes in academic status that interrupt a student's enrollment often include: Withdrawal (in course); Suspension; Dismissal; Suspension or Dismissal for Academic Misconduct; Disciplinary Suspension; or Disciplinary Dismissal (or equivalent terms).

See Glossary. See also discussion in Chapter Five, "Recording Academic and Disciplinary Actions on Transcripts."

DATABASE Essential
TRANSCRIPT Not Recommended

Academic Suspension or Ineligibility to Re-enroll

Essential to database. For further discussion see Chapter Five.

DATABASE Essential
TRANSCRIPT Optional

Disciplinary Suspension or Ineligibility to Re-Enroll

Essential to database. For further discussion see Chapter Five.

DATABASE Essential
TRANSCRIPT Not Recommended

Academic Honors in Progress

Institution-wide academic honors—not departmental honors or organizational memberships—awarded during a student's career may, at the institution's option, be recorded in the database or on the honors transcript. See also, "Honors and Distinctions."

DATABASE Optional
TRANSCRIPT Optional

Rank in Class

Student's rank in class where 1 = highest rank. Several factors that render class rank less precise or consistent than it seems: Variations in grading practices among the faculty at an institution or from one institution to another; variations in methodologies used to define a class, *e.g.*, all those graduating on a particular date, meaning there may be several classes in a given year, or all those graduating within a 12-month period; and variations in methodologies used to calculate rank, *e.g.*, whether or not plusses and minuses with differing point equivalents are used to modify letter grades and whether or not ranks are recalculated if a grade change is recorded after the initial rankings. Since such factors are less likely to remain inarticulated in professional schools, the use of class rank as a tool may be more appropriate to professional schools such as medicine and law.

DATABASE Optional
TRANSCRIPT Not Recommended

Statement of Graduation

Degree Received

Title of degree.

DATABASE Essential
TRANSCRIPT Essential

Date Conferred

Date the degree is officially awarded. While the month and year are essential, inclusion of the day of the month is also recommended.

DATABASE Essential
TRANSCRIPT Essential

Date Completed

Should be included if different from the date of the degree conferral. Should be reflected on the transcripts of those institutions which do not confer degrees at the end of the term in which the student completes degree requirements. While the month and year are essential, inclusion of the day of the month is also recommended.

DATABASE Essential
TRANSCRIPT Recommended

Major

The institution's name for the major field of study is essential.

NOTE The CIP (Classification of Instructional Programs) code should be considered Essential for the database and Optional for the transcript.

NOTE The major should appear on the transcript, but not on the diploma.

DATABASE Essential
TRANSCRIPT Essential (as major);
CIP code is optional

Minor

A prescribed number of courses, usually about half of the number required for the major, in an academic discipline. (See Glossary under "Minor Area of Study.")

DATABASE   Essential
TRANSCRIPT   Essential

Honors and Distinctions

These should be limited to academic graduation honors and should not include membership in honorary organizations or other nonacademic distinctions and awards. See also "Academic Honors in Progress."

DATABASE   Essential
TRANSCRIPT   Recommended

Professional Certification Requirements

Include only if part of degree requirements; specific test scores should not be reflected.

DATABASE   Recommended
TRANSCRIPT   Optional (unless state law or professional licensing requires placement on the transcript)

Supplemental Information for Graduate and Professional Students

Satisfactory Completion of Institutional Qualifying Examinations

DATABASE   Essential
TRANSCRIPT   Optional

Advancement and/or Admission to Candidacy

DATABASE   Essential
TRANSCRIPT   Optional

Title of Thesis or Dissertation

DATABASE   Optional
TRANSCRIPT   Optional

Transcript Issuance Information

COURSES IN PROGRESS

List of courses in which the student is enrolled at the time of issuance of the transcript. May be very helpful to potential employers, colleges, universities, and professional schools to which the student may be applying. "In Progress" should be clearly noted. For schools using an "early registration" procedure, preregistered courses should not be included on the transcript until classes have begun. If the list of current courses is not shown, then the transcript may indicate whether the student is currently enrolled.

DATABASE   Essential
TRANSCRIPT   Optional

DATE OF ISSUE

Necessary in order for the recipient to know if the record received is current. Sending information should be maintained for a period of time as an audit trail in compliance with FERPA requirements.

DATABASE   Optional
TRANSCRIPT   Essential

Last Entry Notation

The recipient can readily determine if data has been entered illicitly.

DATABASE   Not Applicable
TRANSCRIPT   Essential

Chapter Four

Key to the Transcript

① ② ③ ❹ ⑤ ⑥ ⑦ ⑧ ⑨ ⑩ ⑪ ⑫

Every transcript should include a key or legend which helps to clarify the information contained in that document and which provides guidance to understanding and evaluating that information. The key should be an integral part of the transcript document—usually printed or photocopied on the back of the transcript paper stock—so that the key will not be separated from the basic document. (The SPEEDE/ ExPRESS transcripts have elements of the key integrated in the data elements and transaction set.)

It is essential that the following items be included in the key if they are not shown on the face of the transcript:

- Name, address, and location of the institution and/ or (if applicable) branch
- Any institutional name changes
- Telephone number of institution or issuing office (identify which)
- Accreditation statement
- Calendar system
- Definition of enrollment terms (specify approximate start and end date or length of term)
- Unit of credit (semester, quarter, other—if other, recommended means of translation to semester or quarter units)
- Grading system (e.g., A=4, B=3, etc.)
- Method of grade point average calculation
- Institutional policy on recording all courses attempted
- Institutional policy on withdrawals, transfer credits, incompletes, repeated courses, academic bankruptcy

- Course identification system indicating level (freshman, sophomore, etc.)
- Explanation of any unique or unusual policies or programs
- Where applicable, dates of changes should accompany each of the above items
- Method of certification as an official transcript (card stock used, embossed seal, etc.)
- A warning against alteration or forgery
- Policy regarding eligibility to re-enroll (e.g., academically eligible to re-enroll unless otherwise noted)
- FERPA re-disclosure statement
- Date of last revision to the key

[21]

The following are optional items that might be included in a key:

- Office to contact for student's disciplinary record Note: Contact counsel to develop a policy before including such an item on the transcript key
- Codes or abbreviations used on transcript
- Institutional ID codes such as FICE, ACT, CEEB, etc. (if included identify which code is being reported)
- Policy on academic probation/suspension
- Graduation requirements
- Degrees awarded by the institution, and their abbreviations (if used)
- Requirements for honors
- Consortium agreements
- Fax number for issuing office or institution (identify which)

Chapter Five

Some Current Issues

①②③④❺⑥⑦⑧⑨⑩⑪⑫

Recording Academic and Disciplinary Actions on Transcripts

Summary: Recommendation and Reasoning

Whether to record academic separations and/or disciplinary separations on the academic transcript is an issue that generates intense discussions. Our recommendations are as follows:

- We recommend that disciplinary separations *not* be recorded on the academic transcript.
- However, we recommend that the option to record academic suspension or "ineligibility to re-enroll" be preserved as an option for the institution.
- Finally, we recommend against noting "ineligible to re-enroll" (non-specific basis) on the transcript.

Our reasoning, in brief: For disciplinary separations, no detailed supporting information is included on the transcript, thus making the notation of separation vague, non-specific, and punitive.

For academic separations, on the other hand, it could be argued that all the necessary detailed supporting factors (grades, GPA, hours earned, semesters enrolled, academic progress) are included on the transcript, thus making a notation on the transcript of academic suspension unnecessary. However, several factors weigh against this conclusion, at least as the sole alternative. First, even with the presence of "keys" to the transcript, not all grading systems are immediately transparent, nor are the academic standards of the institution always clearly stated—*i.e.*, what is the minimum grade point average necessary to continue. Moreover, even if the transcript made those factors clear, institutions that process many transcripts may particularly appreciate a clear statement from the sending institution as to the academic status of the student in question. Hence the divergence in our recommendations.

After a brief review of both historical developments and current practice, we will explore the logic for not recording disciplinary separations, but for allowing the recording of academic separations on the transcript, at the option of the institution.

Historical Perspective

Historically, schools recorded all "ineligibility to enroll" on permanent record cards. Once recorded, such ineligibility necessarily had to be communicated as a part of the transcript, because (as we explain in the "Historical Perspective" in Chapter Two), the record and the transcript were the same document.

In modern student records systems, however, recording an action and producing it as a part of the transcript are two separate actions. Beginning in the early 1970s, when information systems made it much easier to generate transcripts separately from the permanent record card, it was no longer necessary to include all academic and disciplinary suspensions on the transcript. Beginning at that time, the notation of disciplinary actions on the transcript was almost immediately removed from recommended best practice. Units dealing with student discipline were able to access information from the database or record card, without needing to resort to the transcript.

In recent years, some have called for a return to presenting disciplinary actions on transcripts, although AACRAO has not endorsed this concept.

Current Practice and Perspective

According to the results of the AACRAO survey of current practice among member schools (2002) (see Appendix A), forty-six percent (46%) do not note academic ineligibility to enroll on the transcript and eighty-four percent (84%) do not note disciplinary ineligibility to enroll. Eight percent (8%) of institutions note ineligibility to enroll without distinguishing academic or disciplinary reasons (and 92% of those note a specific time period for ineligibility). Among all responding schools, there were few or no differences in the profile of responses between types of schools (private/public; two-year/four-year/"four plus" years; and small, medium, or large enrollment) in use of the notation "ineligible to enroll" upon the transcript.

In addition, in a companion survey of what AACRAO members felt should be the best practice in their institutions, 29 percent felt that academic ineligibility should not be reported on the academic transcript; 61 percent felt that disciplinary actions should not be reported on the academic transcript; and 74 percent felt that a non-specific notation of "ineligibility to enroll" would be inappropriate.

In short, the results of the survey on current institutional practice indicate a wide range of positions, with a majority of institutions recording academic ineligibility and a very large majority not recording disciplinary ineligibility. The views on best practice follow a similar, but weaker pattern.

Discussion of Recommendations

Our recommendations derive from considerations of both the historic background and current practice. These considerations have been fortified with a concern for current directions in both the integrity of records, and student service.

ACADEMIC INELIGIBILITY TO RE-ENROLL

Whether a student is academically able to re-enroll depends upon the policy and practice of the transcript-issuing institution. For the reasons set forth above, it can be a legitimate option for the sending institution to note that a student is on an academic suspension, or "academically ineligible to re-enroll," so as to eliminate guesswork on the part of the receiving institution. Other institutions, however, believe that all the information necessary to apply that institution's policies concerning academic performance—including the ability to re-enroll—is included on the transcript. Such institutions thus tend to consider that the actual notation of "academic suspension" on the transcript is unnecessary, indeed redundant.

Either position is defensible; hence our recommendation that the notation on transcripts of academic ineligibility to re-enroll be available as an option—according to the policy and culture of the institution.

In any event, in the case of an application to transfer or re-apply, the receiving school should examine the academic record to see if the student would be eligible to continue under its own eligibility standards.

DISCIPLINARY INELIGIBILITY TO RE-ENROLL

The question of placing disciplinary ineligibility to enroll on the academic transcript poses a different dilemma.

We have noted that some schools believe it is unnecessary to place a notation of "academic ineligibility to re-enroll" on the transcript because all of the information necessary to make a judgment is already, ostensibly, on the document. However, for contrary reasons, it is inappropriate to place disciplinary ineligibility on the academic transcript—because usually no information, or inadequate information, is available on the transcript to distinguish the nature or severity of the disciplinary action. Students who are deemed ineligible to re-enroll because of relatively minor offenses would be lumped together with students who have committed far more egregious offenses.

Students use the transcript throughout their lives for employment. They would be branded without a specific charge and therefore without any real hope of refutation. Placing the burden on the transcript of weeding out "bad actors" from the academy reflects an over-reliance upon the tools with which we are familiar and an under-reliance upon alternative solutions. "When your only tool is a hammer, pretty soon all your problems begin to look like nails."

The weeding out function can most effectively be included in the admissions process via direct contact—perhaps a requirement of a good conduct letter or a letter of recommendation—with the disciplinary office of previous schools.

Use of Social Security Numbers:
*in the Student Database; on the
Academic Transcript; as a Student ID;
and for Financial Aid Programs*

Background on the Current Debate

For many years, the Social Security Number (SSN) has been accepted almost without question as a means of identifying students—certainly in the database and on the transcript, and (with more controversy) as an identifying number on student identification cards.

Today the debate is sharply focused; both sides are concerned with fraud. The use of the SSN identifies each student distinctively, and thus helps to prevent fraud, but paradoxically, its use may also facilitate "identity fraud."

Current Practice:
Results of AACRAO Survey of Current Practice

IN THE DATABASE

The survey found, in the spring of 2002, that:

■ Over 90 percent of institutions responding used SSNs as the primary or secondary key in their student academic database;

■ 50 percent of institutions responding use SSNs as their primary student identification in student academic data; and

■ 41 percent use them as the secondary student ID (*i.e.*, SSNs are used in academic data, but not as a basis for awarding student ID numbers).

ON THE TRANSCRIPT

The survey found that:
■ 79 percent of institutions do use the SSN on transcripts;
■ 16 percent do not;
■ 2 percent allow students the option; and
■ 1 percent use a truncated SSN on the transcript.

AS A STUDENT ID

50 percent of responding institutions reported that they currently use the Social Security Number as the Student ID.

FOR GOVERNMENT PROGRAMS

It goes without saying that when a government program requires identification of students by SSN, institutions comply.

The AACRAO survey revealed that 6.7 percent of responding institutions make use of the SSN only for government-mandated purposes.

Recommendations

The best way to make sense of the debate is to distinguish among these four different uses of the SSN: in the student database; on the academic transcript; as a student ID; and for financial aid and other government programs.

AS THE SECONDARY STUDENT IDENTIFIER IN THE DATABASE: ESSENTIAL

Regulations implementing Section 6050S of the Internal Revene Code require institutions to collect and report SSNs for all students on whose behalf tuition is paid. In addition, this use of the SSN provides a convenient check on the student's identity, especially for common or recurring names. It also facilitates interface with external entities such as government agencies, other schools, and testing companies.

AS THE PRIMARY STUDENT IDENTIFIER IN THE DATABASE: NOT RECOMMENDED

Making the Social Security Number the primary identifier in the database makes the SSN available to an unnecessarily wide swath of the campus community.

AS THE NUMBER ON THE STUDENT ID CARD: NOT RECOMMENDED

This use makes the student's SSN number available, without security, throughout the campus and the com-

[27]

munity, increasing the risk of identify theft. Other types of identifiers or passwords are available.

ON THE TRANSCRIPT: RECOMMENDED

The academic transcript is a confidential document whose release has been approved by the student. Use of the SSN on the transcript eases the appropriate sharing of information, and makes fraudulent misappropriation of the student's identity harder to accomplish.

State Law

State law may either require or forbid the use of Social Security Numbers in certain contexts.

Name Change Recommendations

There are two major considerations involved in implementing name changes: on the one hand, the desire to accommodate student wishes; on the other hand, the need to safeguard the integrity of the transcript. There are two additional considerations which may also factor in: state law, and the configuration of your Student Information System.

The following are commonly-occurring situations.

Current Students

Recommendation: All currently-enrolled students should be granted the opportunity to change their names on institutional records upon the production of evidence showing that the student's name has officially changed.

What type of documentation?
- Certified copy of a marriage license, court order, or dissolution decree reflecting the new name in full; or
- Especially for non-U.S. citizens: Current passport or official proof of identity, certified by U.S. embassy abroad or by the appropriate foreign embassy in the U.S.

NOTE AACRAO conducted a survey in the spring of 2002 to discover what was common practice among responding AACRAO registrars, concerning documentation required for making name changes (See Appendix A). The survey revealed that, of the approximately 1,000 respondents to the survey, 30 percent were making name changes based on presentation of a Social Security card, driver's license, or both. And nearly 20 percent were making name changes without requiring any documented proof of name change. Aside from making minor changes in name that are of a ministerial nature (see "Minor Variations in Names" on the next page), AACRAO recommends requiring documented proof of name change based on the documents set forth above.

Former Students

- Recommendation as to transcript and diploma: No name change on the transcript, or on the diploma, except when there has been a court-ordered change of name. Upon presentation of a certified copy of the court order, diplomas in the new name may be issued at the expense of the graduate.

- Recommendation as to database: Carry and use the new name, upon showing of proper documentation. Especially useful for integrated data systems (for example, alumni development wishes to address graduate by most current name).

- Some considerations where the record pre-dates online entry: Records archived on microfilm or microfiche, where the original documents have been destroyed in the normal course, are difficult to change. In addition, some states prohibit, without lawful authority, tampering with or altering of existing records, including expunging critical information.

Re-applicants

Not only the database, but the transcript, can carry the new name.

Gender Changes

A certified copy of a court order is usually required if a change in gender and name is to be recorded on a student's record. Consult with counsel concerning the requirements of state law, if applicable.

Because of the significance of gender change, even records of noncurrent students should be changed, provided the certified copy of the court order has been received and a cross-reference system is in place. No historical evidence of the gender change should be included on the transcript. For new name on diploma, see "Reissuance of Diploma Upon Change of Name, or Change of Gender" below.

Minor Variations in Names

The registrar has discretion to accept minor changes in names (*e.g.*, spelling corrections or revisions). In such instances, the student may be expected to provide documentation such as a current driver's license with photo, Social Security card, or resident alien card.

Reissuance of Diploma Upon Change of Name, or Change of Gender

A diploma may be reissued for a graduate whose name has legally changed. To protect the institution and continuity of records, the new diploma should have special wording printed on its face as follows:

> *Original diploma awarded at Central City on __(date)__. Upon request of the awardee, this diploma was issued following a legal change of name.*

The reprinted diploma should carry the precise date the degree was originally awarded and the date of reissue, but for practical purposes the signatures of the officials should be of those currently in office.

A gender change is almost always accompanied by a name change. In such a case, the phrase above will provide the necessary record continuity without specifically mentioning the gender change.

(Quann, 1994)

Replacing a Lost or Destroyed Diploma

A similar procedure should be followed when a diploma is reprinted to replace an original that has been lost or destroyed. The wording, however, should be slightly different:

> *Diploma awarded at Central City on __(date)__. Upon request of the awardee, this document was reissued on __(date)__ to replace the original that was lost or destroyed* (Quann, 1994).

Replacing a Diploma After an Institutional Name Change

In such a case the suggested wording may be:

> *Degree granted by Central State College on __(date)__. Upon request of the awardee, this document was reissued on __(date)__ to replace the original which was lost or destroyed. This institution officially became Central State University on __(date)__.*

Quann (1994) states: "The special phrasing suggested above may be printed in smaller type, but the print style should match the larger print. These phrases should appear in the body of the diploma so the statement becomes an essential part of the document, not easily covered by a mask or frame."

Quann (1994) adds: "Whenever possible, the replacement diploma should not be released until the original has been returned."

Cross Referencing

Records officers should have a well designed cross-referencing system. This protocol accommodates official name changes for current students, indicating former and new legal names and matching student identification or Social Security Numbers. This precaution is important since staff members tend to come and go, and policies and statutes are subject to change (Quann, 1994).

[30]

Chapter Six

FERPA, USA PATRIOT Act, and Their Impact on Release of Student Education Records

①②③④⑤⑥⑦⑧⑨⑩⑪⑫

The following information is provided as a basic orientation to two of the most important federal statutes that regulate what kind of information from student records can be made available—some with and some without the student's consent. Those two statutes are:

■ FERPA, or the Family Educational Rights and Privacy Act of 1974, as amended, also known as the "Buckley Amendment;" 20 USC 1232g and regulations at 34 C.F.R. Part 99; and

■ USA PATRIOT Act of 2001 (H.R. 3162) (signed October 25, 2001) ("Uniting and Strengthening America by Providing Appropriate Tools Required to Intercept and Obstruct Terrorism").

Resources

The *AACRAO 2001 FERPA Guide* provides a more complete guide to FERPA. The Resources section at the end of this chapter lists additional sources of guidance on FERPA, and the "Compliance" section of the AACRAO Web site posts advisories on compliance on an ongoing basis.

Other Considerations

In addition, bear in mind:

Your *institution* may have committed itself to certain policies that go beyond what FERPA requires (such as a faster turn-around time for release of student information than the 45 days mandated under FERPA).

Your *state* may have enacted one or more privacy statutes that might apply to private as well as public institutions in the state.

And there are other federal statutes that require the release of personally identifiable student information. One example: the Solomon Amendment (allowing personally identifiable "student recruiting information" to be released to military recruiters—including information that might have been denied to them under FERPA). See The *AACRAO 2001 FERPA Guide*, pp. 8, 41–43, and 191-199. Another example: the Campus Sex

Crimes Prevention Act of 2000 (CSPCA) [amends FERPA to clarify that disclosure of information about registered sex offenders attending or enrolled in institutions of higher education (IHEs) is not a violation of FERPA. The burden is on sex offenders to report their student or employment status; on the states to add that information to their databases; and on IHEs to publicize, to their campus community, how such a database can be accessed or found. Notice of compliance is to be appended to compliance with the Campus Security Act of 1990 as of October 1, 2003.]

General Recommendation

We recommend that in dealing with novel or ambiguous situations, or in trying to develop general policy, you consult with in-house or other counsel.

Major Features of FERPA

What Institutions are Covered by FERPA?

FERPA applies to any educational institution that receives funds under any program (including federal student aid) administered by the U.S. Department of Education. (The law also applies to K-12 education.)

Major Rights Safeguarded by FERPA

Confidentiality (right of the student to control disclosure of some records), and *access* (inspection and review of "education records"—any record "personally identifiable" to the student, and maintained by the institution or a party acting for it). Records covered by FERPA include far more than the transcript; they can be generated, and housed, in a broad spectrum of offices across campus. Both confidentiality and access have exceptions, some of which are presented below.

What About Parents?

We will refer throughout this section to the student's rights under FERPA. However, in certain situations, the FERPA rights of students transfer to parents. See The

[33]

AACRAO 2001 FERPA Guide, sec. 5.20 at 28. The Guide "strongly recommends" that "a statement of the institution's policy regarding parental access and disclosure be clearly stated in its FERPA policy."

"Directory Information"— An Exception to Confidentiality

■ What is it? This is open or public information that the institution can release without the written consent of the eligible student—unless the student directs in writing that all or part of his/her directory information be withheld. See 34 CFR 99.37 and 99.30. Directory information is "information contained in an education record of a student that would not generally be considered harmful or an invasion of privacy if disclosed." 34 CFR sec. 99.3. It typically includes, but is not limited to, the student's name, address, telephone listing, e-mail address, and enrollment status (undergraduate or graduate, full- or part-time). See 34 CFR 99.3 (under "Definitions— Directory information") for a listing, which is not exhaustive, of categories of information that could be considered directory information.

■ *Requirement of annual notification to students in attendance of what the institution has designated as directory information*—The institution can designate types of information beyond what are named in the regulations, but it must make an annual public notification of what those categories are. See 34 CFR 99.37. The annual notification must also include a time limit within which eligible students can place a "hold" on their directory information. See 34 CFR 99.37.

■ *Method of notification*—Is left up to the institution, as long as it is reasonably likely to reach all students. Multiple methods may be used. Notification by Web site is acceptable as one of the methods—but only if all students are required to have personal computers, and if those computers have connectivity to the institution's Web site.

■ The following types of information should *not* be included as directory information: Social Security Number or student ID number; race, ethnicity, or nationality; gender; or grades.

When Even Non-directory Information can be Released Without the Consent of the Student

Under certain exceptions as codified by law, records can be released to the following persons or entities without the consent of the student: Personnel within the institution ("school officials" whom the institution has determined have a "legitimate educational interest"); other institutions in which students seek to enroll; persons or organizations providing financial aid to students; accrediting agencies carrying out their accreditation function; organizations conducting studies for the institution; as a response to a request pursuant to a judicial order or lawfully issued subpoena; and in an emergency to protect the health or safety of students or other persons. See 34 CFR 99.31 and 99.36. On subpoenas, see also *The AACRAO 2001 FERPA Guide* at 8, 38–42, and 85–87. Institutions are responsible for informing parties to whom personally identifiable information is released that the recipients of such information are not permitted to disclose the information to others without the written consent of the student. See 34 CFR 99.33 (redisclosure of information).

"Peer Grading"

In *Owasso Independent School District v. Falvo*, 534 U.S. 426 (2002), the Supreme Court ruled unanimously that the grades students give each other in the classroom practice of "peer grading" are not "education records" that are protected under the FERPA statute. Because the court in Owasso found that FERPA did not apply to the case, the justices did not need to resolve the question of whether the private lawsuit was properly brought. (In another case that term, *Gonzaga v. Doe*, the Court ruled that there is in fact no private right of action under FERPA. (See "Enforcement" below.)

Pursuant to Court Order under the USA PATRIOT Act ("the Act") *["Uniting and Strengthening America by Providing Appropriate Tools Required to Intercept and Obstruct Terrorism" Act (Oct. 25, 2001)]*

When the U.S. Attorney General (or any federal officer or employee, in a position not lower than an Assistant Attorney General) certifies that "specific and articulable facts" support the request, such an official may obtain a court order that requires an educational institution to turn over education records related to a terrorism investigation, and the institution does not violate FERPA by complying with such an order, without student consent. See Section 507. The Act also provides that a college or university "shall not be liable to any person" for good-faith disclosure of education records in response to such an order. Note that, as of this printing, the USA PATRIOT Act does not explicitly amend FERPA's "health or safety emergency" exception. See 34 CFR 99.36.

Record of Disclosure

Records of disclosures and requests for disclosures of the student's academic record (other than to the student; to others in response to written requests from the student; or to school officials) are considered a part of the student's academic record and must be retained as long as the academic record is retained by the institution. See 34 CFR 99.32.

Right to Review Education Records

Students must be given the opportunity to review and challenge their "education records." See 34 CFR 99.10. Both currently enrolled and former students have the right to inspect and review their records, and to challenge contents they believe are inaccurate or misleading. However, only currently-enrolled students must be notified (annually) of their right to do so. The institution must comply with a request for access to records "within a reasonable period of time, but not more than 45 days after it received the request." See 34 CFR 99.10.

NOTE If an institution has committed itself to a faster turnaround, that shorter commitment date is what governs.

Right to Challenge Education Records

Students have the right to request to have education records corrected that they believe are inaccurate, misleading, or in violation of their privacy rights. A full and fair opportunity must be provided to present evidence relevant to the issue raised. Students who are not satisfied with the outcome of the challenge process have the right to place in their education record a statement commenting on the contents of the education record, or on their reason for disagreeing with the decision of the hearing panel. See 34 CFR 99.20, 99.21, and 99.22.

Enforcement

Institutions that have a policy or practice of violating FERPA risk having their federal funds withdrawn. In *Gonzaga v. Doe* (No. 01-679) (2002), the Supreme Court ruled that there is no private right of action under FERPA. In other words, enforcement of FERPA lies with the U.S. Department of Education, and its ability to cut off federal funding, if necessary.

Chapter Seven

Transcript Services

Issuing Transcripts

General Considerations

Issuing transcripts is a primary responsibility of the office of the registrar. It is an essential service to the student. Well organized and easily understood transcripts project an image that inspires confidence in the office of the registrar and in the institution as a whole.

Turnaround Time

Prompt transcript service is a hallmark of efficient operation of the office of the registrar. While it is recognized that such service may be slowed during rush periods, the goal should be to produce official transcripts within one working day from the time the request is received. Normal turnaround time should be clearly posted in the registrar's office and printed on the request form.

Recommended: Have a Written Statement Outlining the Institution's Policies Concerning the Release of Transcripts

A number of institutions and agencies specify the manner in which transcript requests should be processed—requests such as: the official transcript must be enclosed with an application; or, a specific number of copies must be included with the application or other documents to be mailed to a third party. Specific processing requests of this type may pose problems for some institutions. Hence, it is recommended that colleges and universities have a written statement clearly outlining the transcript release procedures for the institution. Institutional transcript release policies should not be subject to process demands imposed by entities external to a given college or university.

If the Institution Ceases Operations

From time to time an institution may be required to close its doors and cease operations. In this event it is the responsibility of the institution to insure that its records are moved to a location available to former students and graduates.

Custodian of Record for Institutions That Have Closed

For those institutions that are charged with the responsibility of maintaining records from an institution that has closed, the following guidelines are suggested:

- All records or documents produced should clearly identify the name of the original institution.
- All documents should be printed on safety paper, preferably with the name of the original institution in the background.
- Documents for the closed institution should not bear the seal of the school maintaining the records.
- A statement should be included in the key or legend verifying the authority of the custodian institution to provide these documents. A sample statement follows:

"At the request of (name of closed school or governing agency), the (name of custodian school) has accepted custody of the academic records of (name of closed school) and has agreed to provide copies of documents contained in those records upon request. The University makes no judgment as to the validity, content, or rigor of any course or program represented on the documents."

Transcript Requests

Technology enables students to request transcripts through a variety of means—telephone, touchtone systems, fax, e-mail, World Wide Web, etc. Many institutions have "outsourced" the transcript request process. These institutions have contracted with an outside vendor to act as the institution's legal agent. The vendor very often collects fees and processes the student's request, sending the information to the institution for transcript issuance. More information on outsourcing can be found on the AACRAO Web site at

[40]

www.aacrao.org/pro_development/outsource.htm (report of the Outsourcing Task Force). In accordance with the Family Educational Rights and Privacy Act of 1974 (FERPA), as amended, transcripts usually are issued only at the request of the student. When requests are made in person, appropriate documentation such as a student ID card, driver's license, or information establishing date of birth, dates of attendance, etc. should be required to verify identity.

FERPA allows the release of transcripts to other educational institutions via telephone and e-mail requests if the issuing institution has a published policy stating such. Telephone and e-mail requests from students generally should not be accepted unless the transcript is being forwarded to another educational institution.

Interest in genealogy and family history has increased requests for transcripts of deceased persons. Because FERPA does not apply to deceased persons, such requests should be handled in a manner consistent with institutional policies.

More detailed information on matters related to FERPA and the release of academic records and information can be found in *The AACRAO 2001 FERPA Guide*, and in the *Final Report NSF—LAMP [Logging and Monitoring Privacy] Project: Identifying Where Technology Logging and Monitoring for Increased Security End and Violations of Personal Privacy and Student Records Begin* (2001). (The LAMP publication is downloadable from the AACRAO Web site, www.aacrao.org.)

Records of student transcript requests, date transcript was issued and to whom, and fee payment, if applicable, should be maintained for up to one year. Students should be notified promptly if their transcripts have not been issued because of indebtedness (or other holds), inability to authenticate the source of the request, etc.

Unified Transcript When Student Has Attended More Than One School Within a University

When a student has attended both undergraduate and graduate or professional divisions within one institution, we recommend that the entire record be included on a single transcript. Partial transcripts, showing only one degree, should not be issued.

Security Features

With the advent of desktop publishing and other related technologies, the selection of paper stock and the associated security features is a critical matter. The stock should utilize a color background with an imbedded pattern, preferably the title of the institution. If photocopied, the pattern should drop out and the word "VOID" should appear throughout the paper. A number of other security features are available from paper vendors, several of whom are AACRAO Corporate members.

The face of each page of the paper transcript should include the following items:

- Certifying officer/registrar's signature
- School seal
- Date of issue
- FERPA redisclosure statement (this should be in the Transcript Key); see Chapter Eight, "Fraudulent Transcripts"
- Statement that the transcript has been "ISSUED TO STUDENT," when applicable
- Physical description of transcript (see Chapter Eight, "Fraudulent Transcripts," for more information.)

If institutional policy permits issuing other than official transcripts, such as a student's or advisor's copy, the nature of the document issued should be clearly indicated on each page. Stamps or print lines such as "NOT AN OFFICIAL TRANSCRIPT" or "UNOFFICIAL TRANSCRIPT" can be changed to "OFFICIAL TRANSCRIPT" by removal of a few letters. Alteration is made more difficult if the message covers a portion of the transcript background print (not course entries).

In order to promote the recognition and proper use of official transcripts, guidelines for fighting academic record fraud should be published and included with transcripts issued to entities other than educational institutions. See Appendix D for guidelines.

Withholding Transcripts

Students may be denied transcript services for financial or other holds. The amount of indebtedness leading to sanction is an institutional decision. However, policies governing student indebtedness that affect transcript issuance must appear in appropriate institutional publications. Ample opportunity must be provided for the right of review guaranteed by FERPA (see Chapter Six), and by open records laws in some states.

The National Association of College and University Attorneys (NACUA) (1995) states that debts to colleges and universities other than educational loans are usually dischargeable in bankruptcy (including library charges for lost or unreturned books), and are thus often voided by a general discharge. NACUA (1995) adds that "it is permissible to deny transcripts when the case is no longer pending before the [bankruptcy] court, and educational debts were not discharged, especially if the underlying obligation is a student loan."

However, as in most matters in which litigation could be anticipated, it is advisable to consult university counsel before deciding whether to withhold the issuance of a transcript in a bankruptcy situation.

Faxing Transcripts

Faxing is a widely used medium for the rapid exchange of records and record information. However, some caution and discretion should be exercised.

Properly signed fax requests for transcripts may be accepted as original documents. Generally, transcripts should not be faxed since the document is unprotected in its transmission and arrival at the destination. Also, it is difficult to verify the identity of the person receiving the fax document.

A faxed transcript may be considered official by the receiving institution subject to its policy, security measures, and validation procedures. Absent these safeguards, the receiving institution should consider a fax copy unofficial and use it only until an official transcript, electronic or paper, is received directly from the originating institution.

More information on faxing can be found in the "AACRAO Fax Guidelines" publication, downloadable from the AACRAO Web site (www.aacrao.org/about/fax.htm). The four-page "AACRAO Fax Guidelines" publication contains a "Table: Recommended List of Faxed Documents To Be Sent or Received."

Chapter Eight

Fraudulent Transcripts

With current desktop publishing and reproduction technologies being widely available, records officers should realize that there is not a paper document required by colleges and universities that cannot be forged, altered, manufactured, or purchased. It is incumbent on admissions and records officers to do everything possible to combat such potential fraud.

The safest and most secure method of data transmission available at this time is electronic data interchange (EDI). All colleges and universities should consider the implementation of this technology on their campuses. (See Chapter Twelve, "Electronic Standards for Data Interchange.")

Since campuses also issue paper transcripts, the following precautions are strongly advised.

Outgoing Transcripts

- Transcripts, either official or unofficial, should be printed on safety/security paper, which makes alteration more difficult.
- Plain paper should be used only for internal institutional documents.
- Necessary institution identification should appear on the transcript.
- The registrar's signature and the institutional seal should be embossed, imprinted, computer-generated, preprinted, or handwritten.

- Transcripts should be sent in an official institutional envelope, marked "Official Transcript."
- Metered postage rather than a postage stamp should be used.
- "Issued to Student" should appear on each page of a transcript issued directly to the student.

Incoming Transcripts

Transcripts received by an institution should be carefully screened to identify the following:

- Illogical data items
- Gaps in attendance
- Erasures and inconsistent type fonts
- Transcript came directly from the institutional records office
- Transcript came in an official institutional envelope
- Postmark is appropriate to the location of the institution
- Institutional postage meter rather than a stamp was used
- Postal cancellation mark on the envelope
- Transcript has a recent date of issue
- Official certification

For more details on the topic of fraudulent transcripts, consult the AACRAO publication *Misrepresentation in the Marketplace and Beyond: Ethics under Siege* (1996).

Chapter Nine

Transcription of Nontraditional Work

Nontraditional Work: An Overview

Both the practice of awarding credit for nontraditional educational experiences and the variation in modes of providing educational experiences within the college environment suggest the need to define different types of credit clearly.

Nontraditional learning has been defined as learning that takes place free of space and time limitations. Developments in technology, including the Internet, e-mail, and the World Wide Web, among others, have greatly facilitated the delivery of education, making education more accessible to more people than ever before.

Some examples of nontraditional types of education are: Experiential learning; credit by examination; independent study; correspondence study; distance learning; and external degree programs. Corporate education and continuing education are also areas that have experienced significant growth.

In this chapter, we identify and describe some of the most common types of nontraditional education, as listed above.

In Appendix C, we give examples of how to transcript those types of nontraditional education.

Usefulness of Developing and Publishing Policies Regarding the Acceptance of Credit Offered in Nontraditional Formats

Colleges and universities should develop and publish policies—with careful attention to the interplay of these policies with institutional missions—regarding the evaluation of traditional learning experiences, and establish appropriate credit equivalencies. A variety of resources are available to assist institutions with evaluation of nontraditional learning, some of which are cited in this chapter. Because this publication is focused on transcription issues, it addresses evaluation insofar as it affects the manner in which nontraditional

learning and any credit equivalencies associated with it might be recorded on the transcript.

Calendar Considerations

Nontraditional education very often does not conform to the standard calendar of the institution. Prior learning may begin or end at any time, without regard to the institution's established semester or other calendar dates. Some nontraditional education such as distance learning may offer learning experiences that are open-ended—that is, students work at their own pace; there is no established end date. Institutions will need to establish policies as to how this type of learning will be transcribed.

From the point of view of transcripts, what is most important is that, if the learning experience is not offered in a standard calendar format, the starting and ending dates of the instruction or the prior learning experience, be clearly indicated.

Varying Methods of Transcription

Nontraditional course credits are sometimes transcripted via nontraditional methods—through the use of a narrative transcript, for example. Because nontraditional educational experiences may vary substantially from those conveyed by traditional methods—including non-classroom as well as classroom experience, for example—it is incumbent upon the registrar to transcript nontraditional education in a manner that allows recipients to make informed and reasonable evaluations of the educational experience.

Please see Appendix C, "Examples of Nontraditional Transcript Entries," for samples of good practice.

Identifying Mode of Delivery; Identifying Origin of the Coursework

The issue of identification revolves around two questions: Noting the mode of delivery of the educational experience, and noting the origin of the work.

■ Mode of delivery: We recommend that the mode of delivery not be noted on the transcript. See fuller discussion under "Distance Learning," below.

■ Origin of the educational experience:

▶ If the source of credit is not from your own institution, the source of that credit should be identified on the transcript. (The only exception might be where there are formal inter-institutional agreements.)

▶ In the case of nontraditional learning at another institution, list all transfer courses accepted for credit, or list only a block of credit?—Whether the receiving institution chooses to list, on the transcript, all courses accepted for credit, or whether it posts only an aggregate amount of credit, from a named institution for a named period of time, is a matter to be set by internal institutional policy. See "Transfer Credits Accepted" in Chapter Three ("Database and Transcript Components").

Various Types of Nontraditional Education

In 1989 the Defense Activity for Nontraditional Education Support (DANTES) published a document entitled: *Problems Faced by Military Personnel In Pursuing Higher Education Programs: A Study with Recommendations*. Adapted from that document are the following brief descriptions of various types of nontraditional education.

Experiential Learning

Knowledge gained through life experiences (employment, apprenticeships, internships, cooperative education, studio arts, field experiences, etc.).

The source of credit for experiential learning should be noted clearly on the transcript so as not to be construed as credit earned in a traditional setting.

Credit by Examination

Assessment through testing. The most familiar exam of this type is the College Level Examination Program (CLEP). Other variations include the Advanced Placement (AP) examinations; DANTES Subject Specialized Tests (DSSTs); and the American College Testing (ACT) Proficiency Examination Program (PEP).

Credits awarded through such testing should be in the database and should also appear on the transcript.

Distance Learning

"Distance learning" consists of courses offered entirely or partly of learning that is web-based, web-enhanced, delivered through interactive video, or in any other way taking place free of space or time limitations.

Distance learning courses should not be identified as such, if they are applied to your degree program(s) like more traditionally-presented courses.

Independent Study

One or more resident courses involving research, field work, etc., taken by a student seeking a traditional degree. The student has a great deal of freedom working under the direct supervision of a faculty member.

"Independent Study" courses may be identified as such, at the discretion of the institution.

Study Abroad

"Study abroad" consists of course experiences in another country (1) covered in a formal study abroad agreement or (2) offered directly by the home institution.

These courses, or a summary of credit earned, should be identified on the transcript as a study abroad experience, including the country of study at a minimum, and if appropriate, the institution attended (*i.e.*, the institution offering the courses in the host country.)

Military Education

GUIDE TO THE EVALUATION OF EDUCATION AND EXPERIENCE IN THE ARMED FORCES

The Commission on Educational Credit and Credentials—formerly known as the Commission on Accreditation of Service Experiences—prepares credit recommendations for learning acquired through military educational experiences.

The Commission works in conjunction with the American Council on Education and AACRAO. The credit recommendations are available in the publication: *Guide to the Evaluation of Education and Experience in the Armed Forces* [the ACE Guide].

FORMS OF MILITARY EXPERIENCE AND EDUCATION, FOR EVALUATION

Military experiences and education may be presented to an evaluator in many forms:

- *Army*: AARTS transcripts (Army/American Council on Education Registry Transcript)
- *Navy*: SMART transcripts (Sailor/Marine American Council on Education Registry Transcript)
- *Air Force*: CCAF transcript (Community College of the Air Force)
  Note: CCAF is a regionally accredited institution that is a depository for Air Force military credit.

DEPARTMENT OF DEFENSE (DD) FORMS

These forms are available to all branches of the service, including the Marines and Coast Guard. Military forms include:

- *DD Form 214* is the Certificate of Release or Discharge from Active Duty for all services. It gives documentation of schools and occupations while in the service.

- *DD Form 295* is an Application for The Evaluation of Learning Experiences during Military Service and is available to all active-duty service members.

- *DD Form 2586 or VMET* (Verification of Military Experience and Training) consists of ACE-recommended credit for military courses attended/occupational skills and training acquired while on active duty and is designed as a transition tool to assist potential employers in the private sector. This form is best used with a DD 214.

- *DD Form 1059* is a Service School Course Completion/Academic Evaluation Report that may be used to complement other records, or when service courses are not recorded on official records such as the DD 214.

- *NAVPERS 1070/604* (Navy Occupational/Training and Awards History), sometimes referred to as "page 4" of the service record, may also be used to supplement other records. The student with a NAVPERS may not be eligible for a SMART transcript.

- *Certificates*—Awarded after the completion of individual courses.

OTHER SOURCES OF MILITARY-BASED EDUCATION

- Defense Language Institute—
  Is regionally accredited
- Defense Equal Opportunity Management Institute
- Defense Acquisition University
- Defense Information School
- U.S. Army Intelligence School

NOTE All of the above are included in the *ACE Guide*.

FURTHER ADVICE ON TRANSCRIPTING OF MILITARY-DERIVED CREDIT: IDENTIFY AS "MILITARY CREDIT" ON THE TRANSCRIPT.

Credit awarded by your institution for military training and/or military experience needs to be clearly

[51]

marked as "Military Credit," with the accompanying information from the *ACE Guide* to include the following: assigned ACE number dates and name of course or experience, and hours awarded.

Special precaution needs to be taken when awarding military credit to ensure that it is not duplicate credit that you have already accepted from a previous institution.

Corporate Education

Business and industry often provide their employees with workplace coursework and training. Very often the employer and the employee would also like to have academic credit awarded for the training provided. Some of the larger programs are accredited, but most are not. In either case, institutions must develop their own standards for review, determining what, if any, corporate training and education they will accept for academic credit—and hence, for posting on the transcript.

The American Council on Education (ACE) provides a service that assists in the review of corporate training and education. CREDIT (College Credit Recommendation Service) replaces a service previously known as PONSI (Program on Noncollegiate Sponsored Instruction).

The term "corporate education" is also used to describe those programs in which an employer contracts with an institution to provide education, often allowing the possibility of earning academic credit.

External Degree Programs

Such programs allow students to bring together credit from a variety of sources, then have it entered on a single transcript and applied to a degree program. Institutions offering external degree programs may or may not offer courses of their own.

Continuing Education

Continuing education provides opportunities for extending education at the postsecondary level. Traditionally the method of providing this education was via off-campus programs, extension centers, evening/weekend programs, and telecourses. With the advent of the Internet and the World Wide Web, continuing education is taking place online and is often closely associated with corporate training. Continuing education programs can be offered for academic credit, or not for credit.

If continuing education is offered for academic credit toward a degree or certificate, it should appear on the transcript.

Continuing education should not be confused with Continuing Education Units (CEU). CEUs are used to maintain certification in many professional fields, but are not included on academic transcripts. See Chapter Ten (Continuing Education Unit Records); see also, definitions in the Glossary.

Chapter Ten

Continuing Education Unit (CEU) Records

The International Association for Continuing Education and Training (www.iacet.org/about/about.htm) defines the Continuing Education Unit (CEU) as the "contact hours of participation in an organized continuing education experience under responsible sponsorship, capable direction, and qualified instruction."

A CEU record corresponds to ten contact hours (60-minute hour) of continuing education. These educational experiences are used to maintain certification in many professional fields.

CEU records serve essentially the same purpose as any other record of educational experience and should be designed to facilitate transcript production. However, they should not be considered analogous to academic course work and are not included on the academic transcript.

An individual record for each participant must be maintained by the sponsoring organization or by the institution's designated CEU record keeping office. An office that is unrelated to those that maintain student academic records frequently performs this function.

NOTE Services for recording CEU on a national basis are available through agencies such as the Center for Adult Learning of the American Council on Education www.acenet.edu/calec/corporate/ceu.cfm.

CEU records should be maintained in a format similar to that of an academic record and may be integrated with academic records in the database. However, academic and CEU transcripts should be issued separately.

The following data elements should be recorded on the CEU transcript:

[55]

- Name and location of sponsoring organization
- Name and ID number of the participant
- Course number (any structured or codified series of numbers that will uniquely identify the CEU program or activity)
- Title of the program or activity
- Date or length of program or activity
- Qualitative or quantitative evaluation of individual's performance
- Number of CEUs awarded (10 contact hours equal one CEU)
- A brief description of the program itself
- Date issued

At the discretion of the sponsoring organization, the following student data elements may be included as transcript items:

- Month and date of birth (essential if the ID number is not used)
- Place of birth
- Home address
- Location of program or activity

NOTE Prior education and employment status of students should not appear on CEU transcripts.

Chapter Eleven

Security of Records

① ② ③ ④ ⑤ ⑥ ⑦ ⑧ ⑨ ⑩ ⑪ ⑫

Elements of a Records Security System

The responsibility for maintaining the security of academic records has increased considerably over the last 35 years. Today, no college or university can rest comfortably with the knowledge that steel file cabinets are safely housing permanent records against fire, theft, and unauthorized access. Most institutions have embraced technologies designed to improve the efficiency and effectiveness of the records operation. Accompanying these new technologies are additional security issues.

To ensure the security of records in an increasingly technological environment, campus security systems must include all of the following elements:

- Identification of modes of record storage and retrieval
- Physical security of buildings and offices housing record storage and retrieval activities
- Security consciousness training for all persons having access to records
- Security of supplies and equipment
- Security of electronic data storage systems
- Security safeguards and challenges, including personal identification numbers (PINs) and other barriers

Identification of Modes of Record Storage and Retrieval

After an initial survey to identify where, how, and by whom data is maintained and accessed, periodic follow-ups must be scheduled to identify any changes in the location or accessibility of data. These security surveys should complement the periodic updates of types and locations of education records required under the provisions of the Family Educational Rights and Privacy Act (FERPA), as amended, as well as by state laws and regulations.

The examination of the security of records is a continuing process. Even after the initial security survey is completed, records security should be addressed, as a matter of routine, on a regular basis.

On most campuses records are stored in many forms, including paper, micrographics, computer machine-readable records, and electronic imaging systems. Identifying the various kinds of record formats (permanent records, grade reports, class rosters, advising reports, graduation checks and transfer credit evaluations) can be daunting because the forms of electronic records have proliferated. The transformation also requires that appropriate security procedures be implemented for each of the various modes in which records can be stored and retrieved. (See *AACRAO's Retention of Records: Guide for Retention and Disposal of Student Records*, 2000.)

Physical Security

Planning and implementation of physical security measures must include not only the principal records office, but all other areas where academic records are maintained and accessible. Planning for physical security must incorporate features that will minimize damage from potential disasters such as fires, floods, tornadoes, and earthquakes. Buildings must be inspected to identify the need for sprinkler and fire alarm systems, elevated storage of paper records, reinforced walls, and stabilization of file cabinets, computers, and other equipment. Taking precautions such as these can make the difference between inconvenience and possibly irretrievable loss.

In addition to modifying physical structures to withstand catastrophes, copies of vital institutional records should be stored off-site in such places as bank vaults, state archive facilities, or other institutions.

Theft and vandalism can be minimized by limiting distribution of keys to offices, storerooms, and equipment, and by limiting knowledge of vault combinations and computer passwords. Procedures should be established to identify persons entering secured areas and to record times of entry and departure. Alarm systems for secure areas should be connected directly to campus security systems to ensure immediate response to any alarm. Another vulnerable area consists of mailboxes, both incoming and outgoing, which are often out in the open and not in a secured space. Wastebaskets can be another area of concern; records waiting for disposal should also be part of the security plan. Ideally, wastebaskets should not be used for disposal of records without pre-shredding the paper.

Answering the following questions will aid the campus assessment of the quality of physical security arrangements:

- Have campus buildings been assessed for structural integrity?
- Has the whole spectrum of systems and equipment been evaluated critically to identify potential hazards?
- Are copies of important documents, including microfilmed records and electronic files, stored at remote sites?
- Have provisions been made for rapid retrieval of back-up materials?
- What security provisions are used during working hours? Are they effective?
- Can unauthorized persons view confidential material or hear confidential conversation(s)?
- How secure are offices after regular working hours? If someone enters through a window or door, will an alarm sound? If so, what will be done?
- Do offices have fire and smoke alarm systems? If a signal is emitted, where is the signal heard or sent? Has the system been tested lately?
- Do staff members know the location of fire extinguishers and fire hoses, and how and when to use them?
- Do staff members have specific assignments in the event of fire or other emergency?

- Who has keys to the office? Have all keys been returned by former employees? When were the locks last changed?
- Are security procedures in effect in the time between office operation and office closure? Are the offices where records are stored designated as secure spaces with limited access at night by other school personnel?
- Has a disaster recovery plan been written? Are copies stored off-site in a secure area?
- Are records professionals aware of computer back-up schedules and storage arrangements?

Security Training for Staff

All persons (including student assistants) having access to personally identifiable data must be made aware of their responsibility for ensuring the integrity of the information.

The following are some practical steps that can enhance staff consciousness of the vital importance of ensuring the confidentiality and integrity of information:

- *Staff training programs*—The importance of maintaining security must be emphasized in staff training programs. This includes not only staff with responsibility for entering and modifying data, but for all other persons having access to such data.

- *Log-on screens and campus-wide publications*—Regular reminders of the responsibility for maintaining data security should be included in campus-wide publications and log-on screens.

- *Affidavits*—All persons with access to personally identifiable data should be required to sign affidavits acknowledging their responsibility for maintaining record security, and recognizing the consequences of security breaches. Department and faculty offices can be particularly vulnerable to unauthorized access to data systems. Data access should be available only to those who need to know.

Do not forget that it is not only members of your staff who have access to the area; cleaning personnel, physical plant employees (such as painters, electricians, etc.), delivery persons, as well as students who come into the area daily, can be a security risk. Cleaning staff and other outside staff who have access to secured spaces should also be required to sign affidavits.

■ *Vigilance*—Reminder of the need for vigilance is especially necessary to counteract bad habits resulting from complacency. Records security may be compromised by staff carelessness resulting from regular use of personally identifiable data. Special efforts must be made to remind staff members to monitor the physical security of the primary records office and to avoid discussing office matters with unauthorized persons. Discussion of students' records, grades, eligibility, etc., must not occur outside the office.

■ *Internal audits*—To enhance records security, internal audits should be conducted on a regular basis. By periodically checking the integrity of academic records, the registrar and others entrusted with maintaining records security can identify breaches in security in sufficient time to rectify problems.

Supplies and Equipment

Security paper, forms, stationery, institutional seals, diplomas, signature and certification stamps, and other supplies and equipment used by staff members to carry out their responsibilities must be located so that the supplies and equipment are not accessible to unauthorized personnel during regular office hours. To thwart pilferage and unauthorized access, these items must be stored in secure locations when not being used, or when the office is closed. Inventory control, distribution, and use of items such as those noted should be assigned to specific staff.

Electronic Data Storage

Maximum-security protection must be designed into computer systems. Although security systems must meet the identified security requirements of the institution, the system must also be sufficiently flexible to provide easy access and update capabilities to support daily operation. Since technology is changing and advancing at a rapid rate, the security system which is suitable for today's needs will not remain adequate indefinitely. Institutions must be willing to allocate resources to continually upgrade security of their electronic data storage. Within the constraints of the institution's budget, it is recommended that there be at least one person with information technology (IT) expertise, either in the registrar's office or in the IT office, part of whose responsibilities include maintaining awareness of new threats to computer security, and new countermeasures available to defeat them.

Back-up materials, including tapes and copies of optical images and microforms, should be stored in secure remote locations as a safeguard against loss resulting from natural disasters, vandalism, or human error. Computer-generated transcripts, letters, certifications, and other critical output should be protected by stringent data processing systems security, well-defined office security techniques, and audit trail processes.

Safeguards and Challenges

The regular testing of all aspects of a security system is necessary to identify flaws. This effort should be ongoing and diligent. The ability to make changes to the academic record should be limited to staff directly responsible for establishing and maintaining the institution's academic records. Strict audit trails on all record entries, and changes of records, must be developed and maintained. A procedure for notifying faculty, chairs, and deans of changes in students' academic status, and grade changes, should be established. E-mails can be used for this purpose, as well as electronic signatures.

[61]

Establishment of personal identification numbers (PINs) for student access to their own records must also be safeguarded against access by inappropriate persons. Students must be made aware of the importance of their PIN, and the need to safeguard their record information from illegal use by others. A pamphlet explaining to students the importance of keeping their record information secure should be a component of students' orientation materials.

All documents containing confidential information must be destroyed when no longer needed, following your campus records retention schedule. Confidential information should never be placed in waste containers or recycling bins. Arrangements should be made to have sensitive documents shredded or otherwise safely destroyed under the supervision of approved personnel, including contracted vendors.

Records professionals should encourage the development of state laws permitting prosecution under criminal codes of persons who make changes to issued transcripts, create bogus transcripts, break the security of data systems, make unauthorized additions/deletions to permanent records, or otherwise alter data in academic records. States are now realizing the seriousness of these crimes, and state laws are rapidly changing. To determine whether a state has such a law, contact the legislative information and research office at the state's capital.

Chapter Twelve

Electronic Standards for Data Interchange: EDI and XML

In addition to fax and mail, there is another means of conveying transcripts: electronically over the Internet. In 1988, the AACRAO Executive Committee appointed a task force to explore the feasibility of creating national standard formats to be used to exchange student transcripts directly between educational institutions using electronic media. The task force is now the AACRAO Standing Committee on Standardization of Postsecondary Education Electronic Data Exchange (SPEEDE).

AACRAO is a member of the Postsecondary Electronic Standards Council (PESC). Established in 1997, PESC is an umbrella group of higher education associations, colleges and universities, software and service providers, and state and federal agencies. PESC develops standards for electronic data-sharing within higher education. It then submits those standards to the American National Standards Institute (ANSI). ANSI is a private, non-profit organization that promulgates voluntary standards, which become accepted across a wide variety of industries.

ANSI has an "Accredited Standards Committee X12" that focuses specifically on standard formats for the electronic exchange of data. SPEEDE and the Postsecondary Electronic Standards Council (PESC) develop formats for such electronic exchanges of student data—formats that can then be approved as standards by Committee X12.

Committee X12 has approved Electronic Data Interchange (EDI) standards for various transactions. Approved EDI standards in education include formats to exchange transcripts; to acknowledge that a transcript was received; to process a request for a student transcript; and to generate a negative response to a request for a transcript.

Another format—using Extensible Markup Language, or XML—is an emerging X12 standard. SPEEDE and PESC are working with X12 to get the XML standard for sending and receiving transcripts approved by ANSI. Such approval will give institutions a choice of two electronic formats for the exchange of student transcripts.

The exchange of student transcripts electronically, by either format, provides several benefits over the exchange of paper documents.

SPEED

In addition to the speed of getting the transcript from one school to another, the principal benefit is realized by the receiving institution's ability to process the electronic document much faster than a paper document. The time involved in opening the mail and entering data from the document into the receiving school's database is eliminated.

SECURITY

Security is greatly improved by this technology. The authenticity of the sending school's transmission is verified by the use of the acknowledgment transaction, which provides evidence that the document came from the school purporting to have sent it; the sending school is also notified of the date of receipt. In addition, the use of the EDI Server at the University of Texas at Austin guarantees that the electronic transcript was in fact sent by the school that claims to have sent it. The acknowledgment process ensures that certain key data elements were received unchanged.

PREVENTION OF FRAUD

Desktop publishing software has facilitated the creation of fraudulent documents. The SPEEDE process provides the most effective way to ensure that the transcript received is authentic and accurate.

ACCURACY

Since information from the transcript does not have to be entered manually into the receiving school's database, the potential for error in data entry is virtually eliminated.

INTERPRETATION OF DATA

Data elements contained in the SPEEDE transcript are clearly defined in the SPEEDE Implementation Guide, which makes it easy to interpret accurately the information received in the SPEEDE format. Definitions and policies usually included in the key to the paper transcript are specified in the SPEEDE Implementation Guide.

Additional information about the SPEEDE standards, process, and the format of the electronic transcript is available in *A Guide to the Implementation of the SPEEDE/ExPRESS Electronic Transcript*, available from PESC, One Dupont Circle, N.W.; Suite 520; Washington, DC 20036, or on the web at www.standardscouncil.org.

Appendix A

Description of Two AACRAO Surveys Concerning
Academic Transcripts and Records

Ⓐ Ⓑ Ⓒ Ⓓ Ⓔ Ⓕ

In the spring of 2002, AACRAO conducted two different surveys of its registrar members. The purpose of the first survey was to find out how institutions are handling the following issues. The purpose of the second survey was to find out the registrar's opinion of "best practices" at his or her institution. Here is a summary of the results.

In each survey, the issues were the same:

■ Notation on the academic transcript of ineligibility to re-enroll—for academic, disciplinary, or non-specific reasons.
■ Use of Social Security Numbers as a student identifier—within the student academic database or on transcripts.
■ Documentation of name changes— What is being required?
■ Use of e-mail for official documentation of administrative academic decisions.

Survey A: Survey of Current Practices

Findings

The focus of each question was: What is the practice of your institution (rather than the personal opinion of the respondent)?

NOTATION ON THE TRANSCRIPT OF INELIGIBILITY TO RE-ENROLL

The survey found that:
■ 84% of institutions do not note "disciplinary ineligibility to re-enroll" on the transcript;
■ 54% do note academic ineligibility to re-enroll.
■ 90% do not note ineligibility to enroll on a nonspecific basis.

USE OF SOCIAL SECURITY NUMBERS

■ As to the use of SSNs in the database, the survey found that:

▶ 50% of institutions responding use Social Security Numbers as their primary student identifier in student academic data;

▶ 41% use them as the secondary student ID (*i.e.*, SSNs are used in academic data, but not as a basis for awarding student ID numbers based on the Social Security Number).

■ In relation to using Social Security Numbers on transcripts, the survey found that:
▶ 79% of institutions do;
▶ 16% of institutions do not;
▶ 2% allow students the option;
▶ 1% use a truncated Social Security Number on the transcript.

NAME CHANGES

When presented with a request for a name change:

■ 51% of responding institutions would do so only upon presentation of legal proof, such as a marriage license or court order;
■ 19% require no documentation;
■ 16% require either a valid driver's license or a valid Social Security card;
■ 5% require both a valid driver's license and a valid Social Security card.

USE OF E-MAIL TO DOCUMENT OFFICIAL ACADEMIC DECISIONS

Finally, when asked whether their institutions use e-mail to document official academic decisions:

■ 47% of registrars said their institutions do not;
■ 25% said that their institutions have no policy on the matter;
■ 18% of institutions allow the practice, but with the proviso that written signatures are required for the most serious decisions.

[69]

Characteristics of the Respondents to the First Survey

NUMBER AND GEOGRAPHICAL DISTRIBUTION OF RESPONDENTS

Nearly half of AACRAO's member institutions responded to this survey. Some 1,036 institutions, or 42% of the total institutional membership, are represented. Respondents came from every state and the District of Columbia.

BREAKDOWN BY INSTITUTIONAL CONTROL:

- 53% were from private (nonprofit) institutions
- 44% were from public institutions
- 3% were from proprietary (private for-profit) institutions

BREAKDOWN BY TYPE OF INSTITUTION:

- 61% were four + years in length (*i.e.*, offering undergraduate, graduate, and/or professional programs)
- 20% were two-year institutions
- 19% were four-year (undergraduate) only

BREAKDOWN BY FULL-TIME UNDERGRADUATE HEADCOUNT ENROLLMENT (2001):

The greatest number of responding institutions had a full-time undergraduate headcount enrollment of 1,000–2,499. The full breakout is as follows:

Enrollment at Responding Institutions	
Headcount	%
Under 500	15.4
500–999	14.3
1,000–2,499	27.1
2,500–4,999	17.2
5,000–9,999	12.5
10,000–19,999	9.0
20,000–29,999	3.1
30,000–39,999	1.0
40,000 or more	0.4

Survey B: Your Opinion of Transcript/ Academic Records Best Practice for Your Institution

Focus of the Second Survey

AACRAO conducted a survey of its members in the spring of 2002 to determine what they viewed to be the best practices for an institution of their type, for the following responsibilities:

- Notation on academic transcript of ineligibility to re-enroll, for academic, disciplinary, or nonspecific reasons;
- Use of Social Security Numbers as a student identifier in the academic database and on transcripts;
- Documentation of name changes;
- Use of e-mail for official documentation of administrative academic decisions.

In each case, the focus of the question was the personal opinion of the respondent.

Summary of Results

NOTATION ON THE TRANSCRIPT OF VARIOUS INELIGIBILITIES TO ENROLL:

Of Academic Ineligibility to Enroll
- 71% of respondents favored the notion of placing "academic ineligibility to enroll" on the transcript;
- Of the 71% majority, 58% of respondents felt that this notation should not be removed even after some specific time limit or when eligibility to enroll is reinstated.

Of Disciplinary Ineligibility to Enroll
- 61% of respondents felt that disciplinary ineligibility to enroll should not appear on the transcript in any form;
- Of the 39% minority, 60% felt that the remark should be removed when eligibility to enroll is reinstated.

Of Non-Specific Ineligibility to Enroll

- 74% of respondents felt that non-specific ineligibility to enroll should not be noted on the transcript;
- Of the remaining 26%, 60% felt that the remark should not be removed when eligibility to enroll is reinstated.

USE OF SOCIAL SECURITY NUMBERS:

In the Academic Database

- 95% of respondents felt that they should use Social Security Numbers in the academic database;
- 49% of those who advocate the use of Social Security Numbers in the academic database felt that ssns should be used only as a secondary identifier;
- 23% of those that advocate the use of Social Security Numbers in the academic database felt that they should only be kept for purposes of mandated government reporting.

On the Transcript

- 72% of respondents felt that they should use Social Security Numbers on transcripts;
- 16% of those that advocate the use of Social Security Numbers on the transcript felt that they should only print a truncated portion;
- 16% of those that advocate the use of Social Security Numbers on the transcripts felt that they should offer students the option whether or not to print the SSN on transcripts.

NAME CHANGES:

Enrolled Students

- 60% of respondents felt that they should only allow for the name change of an enrolled student if the student presents legal evidence of name change, such as a marriage license or court order;
- Of the remaining 40%, 56% would allow the name change of an enrolled student if presented with a valid driver's license or Social Security card;
- Only 0.1% would not change the name of an enrolled student under any circumstances.

Previously Enrolled Students

- 49% of respondents felt that they should only allow for the name change of an enrolled student if the student presents legal evidence of name change, such as a marriage license or court order;
- Of the remaining 51%, one-third would allow the name change of an enrolled student if presented with a valid driver's license or Social Security card;
- 19% of respondents would not change the name of an enrolled student under any circumstances.

USE OF E-MAIL TO DOCUMENT OFFICIAL ACADEMIC DECISIONS:

Between academic offices

- 46% felt that their institution should use e-mail to document some administrative academic decisions, but should require written signature for the most serious academic decisions;
- 19% felt that their institution should not use e-mail under any circumstances to document administrative academic decisions.

Between academic offices and students

- 49% felt that their institution should use e-mail to document some administrative academic decisions, but should use traditional mail for the most serious academic decisions;
- 29% felt that their institution should not use e-mail under any circumstances to document administrative academic decisions.

Characteristics of Respondents

Responses were received from 1,425 institutions representing 57% of total institutional AACRAO membership. Respondents came from every state, the District of Columbia, u.s. territories, and nations abroad.

We tabulated the distribution of responses by control of institution, type of institution, locality, and size. The breakdown by category is as follows:

[71]

BY INSTITUTIONAL CONTROL

- 50% from public institutions
- 46% from private, not-for-profit institutions
- 4% from proprietary institutions

BY TYPE OF INSTITUTION

- 55% from institutions awarding undergraduate degrees as well as professional or graduate degrees
- 21% from institutions offering two-year degrees
- 16% from institutions offering only four-year degrees
- 8% from institutions offering only graduate or professional degrees

BY LOCATION

- 40% from institutions classifying themselves as urban
- 34% from institutions classifying themselves as suburban
- 26% from institutions classifying themselves as rural

BY 2001 FULL-TIME UNDERGRADUATE HEADCOUNT ENROLLMENT

Enrollment at Responding Institutions	
Headcount	%
Under 500	16%
500–999	11%
1,000–2,499	26%
2,500–4,999	16%
5,000–9,999	13%
10,000–19,999	12%
20,000–29,999	4%
30,000–39,999	1%
40,000 or more	1%

Self-Audit

Ⓐ Ⓑ Ⓒ Ⓓ Ⓔ Ⓕ

The *Academic Record and Transcript Guide* is AACRAO's response to the need for consistency in transcripts produced by postsecondary institutions. This self-audit and the sample transcripts included in Appendices C and E provide a practical structure within which to implement the recommendations of the Academic Record and Transcript Guide Task Force.

We recommend that institutions periodically conduct the following self-audit. All staff members of the office of the registrar, and appropriate representatives from other offices, should be included in the audit.

Does your transcript include all of the components listed as essential in Chapter Three of the Guide:

- Name, address, telephone number and Web site of the institution?
- Date of issue?
- Full name of student?
- Name and location of colleges or universities previously attended?
- All courses attempted, with unsatisfactory grades as well as satisfactory grades shown?
- Course type and level clearly identified?
- Amount, unit of credit, and grade for each course?
- Terms of attendance?
- Type of credit clearly labeled, if credit is awarded for non-classroom experiences such as military experience, life experience (experiential learning), and nationally standardized or institutional examinations?
- Statement of graduation containing:
  - ► Degree earned?
  - ► Major, minor and/or program?
  - ► Date degree completed, if different from conferral date?
  - ► Date degree conferred?

Do you ensure that the following are *not* included on your transcripts:

- Information listed as "not recommended" in Chapter Three (Database and Transcript Components)?
- Institutional nonacademic information (sanctions for indebtedness, record of transcripts sent, etc.?)

Is your transcript easy to interpret:

- Are the abbreviations used for course titles understandable?
- Are transfer credit summaries or equivalencies clearly labeled?
- Are graduation data easily located on the transcript?

Are policies and procedures for transcript services effective:

- Is the normal turn-around time as short as possible?
- Do you periodically check your paper transcript for print and copy quality?
- Do the official seal, signature, and date of issue appear on each page of the transcript?
- Do your publications identify the conditions under which a student may be denied transcript service?
- Does a "Key to the Transcript" accompany each official transcript and does it contain the items listed in Chapter Four (Key to the Transcript)?
- Are your academic records and transcript policies in accord with the provisions of FERPA? (See Chapter Six.)

Are your records and transcripts secure:

- Have you recently reviewed the physical security of your office?
  - ► Do you have security procedures in effect during office hours?
  - ► Are confidential materials and conversations protected from unauthorized persons?

- ► Is the office secure from unauthorized entry when closed?
- ► Does the office have burglar and fire alarm systems?
- ► Do the staff members have specific tasks assigned to them in the event of fire or other emergency situations?
- ► Have the locks on the office doors been changed in the past two years?
- ► Do you know what persons have keys to the office?
- ► Is there a security procedure in effect at closing time?
- ► Has a disaster recovery plan been written, and are copies of the plan stored off-site?

- ■ Are there ongoing programs to keep the staff security-conscious?
- ■ Do staff and student workers sign a statement of confidentiality?
- ■ If you use safety paper, is it stored in a safe and secure location?
- ■ Are supplies and equipment used to generate official documents kept in a secure area?
- ■ Are permanent academic records backed up and stored in another building?
- ■ Are there adequate security measures for electronically stored data?
- ■ Do you regularly challenge your own security system?
- ■ Do you follow the guidelines in Chapter Eleven (Security of Records)?

Appendix C

Examples of Nontraditional Transcript Entries

A B C D E F

Experiential Learning

Full Entry

Provide: Date, hours awarded, class level, narrative description, as follows:

Example:

```
October 31, 1993 Four hours (lower level)
```

Narrative Description: Credits granted for prior learning in Adolescent Counseling and Adolescent Development 1991–92 Tri-state youth program, Jackson, Mississippi. Counselor in resident staff.

Responsibilities included supervising recreational activities, intervening in crisis situations, developing daily living skills, and maintaining records.

One-line Entry *(with notation that credit is for experiential learning)*

Example:

```
Fall 1994 Experiential Learning in Criminal
Justice 12 credits (lower level)
```

Entry Showing Institution's Own Courses for Which Equivalent Credit is Granted

Provide: Title of course; date credits awarded; and notation that credit is for experiential learning (the title can designate this); and number of credits awarded, as follows:

Example:

```
AJ 200 Experiential Learning in Criminal
Justice Fall 2002 12 credits
```

Credit by Examination

Notation Not Showing Grade or Course Equivalent at Home Institution

Provide: Credit by examination, test name (CLEP, AP, DANTES, Department, College, etc.), date test was administered, number of credits awarded by institution, as follows:

Example:

```
Credit by Examination:
CLEP (June 21, 2003) US History 3 credits
(lower level)
```

Notation Showing All the Above, Plus Number of Credits and Course Equivalent

Provide: Credit by examination, test name, date test was administered, number of credits awarded by institution, course for which equivalent credit was granted, and notation as to satisfactory grade:

Example:

```
Credit by Examination:
CLEP (June 21, 2003) US History 3 credits
HIST 210
```

Independent Study

Provide: Course number, course title (usually with Independent Study in the title), hours, and grade.

Example:

```
History 400: Studies in the American Civil War
(Independent Study); 3 hours; Grade: A
```

Correspondence Study

See comments on "Distance Learning," next.

Distance Learning

We recommend that courses should not be noted as correspondence, distance, or Internet on the transcript. Follow your normal procedure for transcripting a course.

Military Education and Training Programs

Provide: Date credit awarded, type of credit (*i.e.*, Military Credit), branch of military, *ACE Guide* number (if used), and equivalent course title and hours:

```
Military Credit          March 5-May 10, 2002
NV 70 90015
First Aid                           2 credits
NV 16060007
Marine Science Technology           3 credits
AF 07090026
Emergency Medical Technician        3 credits
```

[80]

Corporate Education

ACE/PONSI (Programs on Noncollegiate Sponsored Education), which has changed its name to ACE/CCRS (College Recommendation Service Program), publishes a reference for the evaluation of Corporate Education.

Full Entry

Provide: Name and location of corporation, course number of ACE/CCRS, title of course, date course taken, number of credit hours, and lower or upper division designation, if there is no course number designation:

Example:

```
February 12, 1999   Microsoft Seattle, WA
COM 200 Millennium 2000 for Networks
3 HRS  Credit
```

NOTE If you use an abbreviation for "corporate," as in "type of credit," it is advisable to add it to the Transcript Key.

One-line Entry

Provide: Notation that class is corporate education; course number; title of course; number of credit hours with notation of satisfactory grade:

Example:

```
Corporate Education: ME 200 Millennium 2000
for Networks  3 HRS  Credit
```

Entry Showing Institution's Own Course for Which Equivalent Credit is Granted

Provide: Title of course; date credits awarded; number of credits awarded; notation that credit is corporate.

Example:

```
CS 230 Corporate Education: Network Servers
Spring 2000 3 Credits
```

External Degree Program

External degree courses should not have any different designations than on-campus courses.

Continuing Education Units (CEUs)

Transcripts for noncredit programs for which CEUs are awarded should be issued separately from those for credit courses. Such a CEU transcript must include the notation that it is a "Continuing Education Unit (CEU) Transcript."

Provide: Name and location of sponsoring organization, course number, title of program, date and length of program, qualitative or quantitative evaluation of individual's performance, number of CEUs awarded, and brief description of program itself:

Example:

```
AACRAO University Washington, DC
Feb. 15-16, 2003
TRAN 111 Transfer Evaluation 1.5 (CEUs)
Satisfactory Participation
A one-day seminar on transcripting
college courses
```

Appendix D

Guidelines for Fighting Fraud

Ⓐ Ⓑ Ⓒ Ⓓ Ⓔ Ⓕ

The following guidelines will help identify and prevent the use of fraudulent academic records. Additional information is contained in the 1996 AACRAO publication *Misrepresentation in the Marketplace and Beyond: Ethics Under Siege*.

What Records Should Be Used

The most complete and protected paper document is the "official" college transcript that has been:

- Issued and mailed directly by the registrar in a sealed institutional envelope.
- Validated with the signature of the registrar and the seal of the institution.

Other letters of certification issued directly by the registrar (and validated) are also relatively secure means of verifying student information.

Unofficial Records

Most records that may have been in the hands of the student—such as student copy transcripts or letters, grade reports, diplomas, or graduation lists—should not be considered official.

What to Look For

Was the document mailed directly from the registrar's office in a sealed institutional envelope using an institutional postage meter (rather than a postage stamp)?

- Is there a registrar's signature and institutional seal, printed or embossed?
- Does the document have a recent date of issue?
- Is the format of the transcript consistent with others received from the same institution?
- Are the records submitted consistent with the person's employment background and with your own personal knowledge of the candidate?

If You Are Suspicious

- Telephone the issuing institution to verify the dates of attendance, degrees granted, and/or honors received.
- Write for more details or return the actual document (or a copy) to the issuing institution for verification.
- If you have received a document other than an official transcript, ask the person to request that an official transcript be sent directly to you.

If a Fraudulent Document Has Been Received

- Notify the issuing institution and return the original, or a copy of the document.
- Report the case to your institutional attorney.
- Inform your local police department.
- Preserve all materials in plastic document holders for latent fingerprints.

What About "Diploma Mills"

Before using any document, make sure that the issuing institution is legitimate. Check to see if it is accredited by an approved agency. If not, investigate further by contacting the Department of Education for the state in which it is located, a state college or university of that state, or the Center for Adult Learning and Educational Credentials, American Council on Education, One Dupont Circle, N.W., Washington, DC 20036.

[83]

Sample Transcript and Key

Ⓐ Ⓑ Ⓒ Ⓓ **Ⓔ** Ⓕ

```
Name          :  Student, A. Good
Student ID    :  111111111
SSN           :  999-99-9999
Birth Date    :  (day/month) 23 May
Print Date    :  2003-01-06 (yyyy-mm-dd)
```

DEGREES AWARDED -

```
Degree       :  Bachelor of Science
Confer Date  :  2002-12-21
Degree GPA   :  3.767
Major        :  Nutrition
```

TRANSFER CREDITS -

DESCRIPTION	HOURS TRANSFERRED
Transfer Credit from SOUTHWEST NEW STATE UNIVERSITY	
Applied Toward Science & Engineering UGRD Program	
Transfer Totals :	16.00
Transfer Credit from NEWER CMTY COLLEGE	
Applied Toward Science & Engineering UGRD Program	
Transfer Totals :	45.00
Transfer Credit from FRESH COUNTY COLLEGE	
Applied Toward Science & Engineering UGRD Program	
Transfer Totals :	13.00
Transfer Credit from WEST OLD A&M UNIVERSITY	
Applied Toward Science & Engineering UGRD Program	
Transfer Totals :	6.00
Transfer Credit from UNIVERSITY OF TORTS	
Applied Toward Science & Engineering UGRD Program	
Transfer Totals :	3.00
Transfer Credit from UNIVERSITY of TORTS	
Applied Toward Science & Engineering UGRD Program	
Transfer Totals :	4.00

BEGINNING OF UNDERGRADUATE RECORD -

2001 Spring Term
Major : B.S.-Nutrition

COURSE		DESCRIPTION	ATTEMPTED	EARNED	GRADE	POINTS
BIOL	20233	Basic Microbiology	3.00	3.00	C	6.000
MANA	30153	Organizational Management	3.00	3.00	A	12.000
NTDT	10211	Nutrition & Weight Control	1.00	1.00	A	4.000
NTDT	30123	Nutrition Thru Life Cycle	3.00	3.00	A	12.000
NTDT	40403	Research Methods In Nutrition	3.00	3.00	A	12.000
THEA	10053	Survey of Theatre Arts I	3.00	3.00	A	12.000
		TERM GPA : 3.625 TERM TOTALS :	16.00	16.00		58.000
		CUM GPA : 3.625 CUM TOTALS :	16.00	96.00		58.000

2001 Summer Term
Major : B.S.-Nutrition

COURSE		DESCRIPTION	ATTEMPTED	EARNED	GRADE	POINTS
SOCI	20213	Introductory Sociology	3.00	3.00	A	12.000
		TERM GPA : 4.000 TERM TOTALS :	3.00	3.00		12.000
		CUM GPA : 3.684 CUM TOTALS :	19.00	99.00		70.000

2001 Fall Term
Major : B.S.-Nutrition

COURSE		DESCRIPTION	ATTEMPTED	EARNED	GRADE	POINTS
NTDT	20113	Issues Of Food In Society	3.00	3.00	A	12.000
NTDT	20363	Comp Appl Fdserv&Ntr Care	3.00	3.00	A	12.000
NTDT	30144	Quantity Food Production	4.00	4.00	A	16.000
NTDT	30303	Overview/Foodser/Nutr Service	3.00	3.00	A	12.000
		TERM GPA : 4.000 TERM TOTALS :	13.00	13.00		52.000
		CUM GPA : 3.812 CUM TOTALS :	32.00	112.00		122.000
		*AACRAO Scholar *Dean's List				

2002 Spring Term
Major : B.S.-Nutrition

COURSE		DESCRIPTION	ATTEMPTED	EARNED	GRADE	POINTS
CHEM	40501	Basic Biochemistry Lab	1.00	1.00	B	3.000
CHEM	40503	Basic Biochemistry	3.00	3.00	C	6.000
NTDT	30313	Food Systems Management	3.00	3.00	A	12.000
NTDT	30333	Medical Nutrition Therapy I	3.00	3.00	A	12.000
NTDT	40363	Community Nutrition	3.00	3.00	A	12.000
RELI	10013	Understnd Rel: World Religions	3.00	3.00	P	6.000
		TERM GPA : 3.461 TERM TOTALS :	13.00	16.00		45.000
		CUM GPA : 3.711 CUM TOTALS :	45.00	131.00		167.000

2002 Fall Term
Major : B.S.-Nutrition

COURSE		DESCRIPTION	ATTEMPTED	EARNED	GRADE	POINTS
NTDT	40333	Medical Nutr Therapy II	3.00	3.00	A	12.000
NTDT	40343	Advanced Nutrition	3.00	3.00	A	12.000
NTDT	40353	Experimental Foods	3.00	3.00	A	12.000
NTDT	40970	Special Problems	1.00	1.00	A	4.000
NTDT	40970	Special Problems	1.00	1.00	A	4.000
		Course Topic(s): Data Collection & Analysis				
		TERM GPA : 4.000 TERM TOTALS :	11.00	11.00		44.000
		CUM GPA : 3.767 CUM TOTALS :	56.00	146.00		211.000
		Undergraduate Career Totals				
		CUM GPA : 3.767 CUM TOTALS :	56.00	146.00		211.000
```

END OF TRANSCRIPT - - - - - - - - - - - - - - - - - - - - - - - - - - - - - - - - - -

Official Academic Transcript
```

AACRAO Sample University

222 University Drive, Washington, D.C. 22222
www.aacrao.edu (222) 111-3333
FICE 555111

Accreditation: AACRAO Sample University is accredited by the Commission on Colleges of the Association of Colleges and Schools to award the Baccalaureate, Master's and Doctoral level degrees. In addition, many of the colleges and academic departments are fully accredited by their individual accrediting agencies. Refer to the University Bulletin for further details (www.Bulletin.aacrao.edu).

Calendar: The academic calendar consists of two long semesters lasting approximately seventeen weeks and one condensed summer semester. Semesters may include several shorter sessions.

Semester Hour: The unit of measure for academic purposes is the semester hour. A semester hour is equivalent to one hour of recitation or a minimum of two hours of laboratory per week for a semester or an equivalent time for a shorter term.

Grading System: ASU uses a four point grading system.

Fall 1995 to Present:

Grade		Quality Points	Used in GPA
A	Excellent	4	yes
B	Good	3	yes
C	Average	2	yes
D	Inferior	1	yes
F	Failure	0	yes
P	Pass	0	no
NC	No Credit	0	no
I	Incomplete	0	no
W	Withdrew	0	no
Q	Dean's Withdrawal	0	no
AU	Audit	0	no
U	Unsatisfactory	0	no

Prior to 1995:

Grade		Quality Points	Used in GPA
A	Excellent	4	yes
B	Good	3	yes
C	Average	3	yes
D	Inferior	1	yes
F	Failure	0	yes
I	Incomplete	0	yes
W	Withdrew	0	no
AU	Audit	0	no

Grade Point Average (GPA): A student's GPA is calculated by dividing the sum of earned quality points by the sum of attempted hours for all courses receiving a grade used in calculating the GPA (see above). Only work taken at ASU is used in the GPA.

Repeated Courses: Prior to Fall 1988 and since Fall 1995 only the grade earned in the most recent repeated course is used in the GPA. In the interim period, for the first three total repeated courses only the most recent grade is used in the GPA; if more than three courses have been repeated, all grades in those courses are included in the GPA.

Withdrawal, Transfer, and Bankruptcy: All attempted coursework appears on the transcript. Students may withdraw up until the midpoint of a semester or session. Transfer work must be university level and earn a grade of at least 'C'. An incomplete becomes an 'F' sixty class days into the subsequent long semester. Students may appeal for academic bankruptcy if they have been separated from the University for at least two years. If granted, all prior coursework will be removed from the GPA and earned hours but will remain on the transcript.

Course Numbering System:

00000–10000	Developmental courses— no credit awarded
10000–29999	Undergraduate lower division courses
30000–49999	Undergraduate upper division courses
50000–59999	Undergraduate and Graduate courses
60000 and above	Graduate Courses

Eligible to Re-Enroll: Academic eligibility to enroll is based upon probation and suspension policies. See Bulletin (ww w.Bulletin.AACRAO.edu).

Transcript Validation and Authenticity: This is an official transcript only if printed on secure purple paper with AACRAO repeated in the background and the official seal of the university on the front of each page. Transcripts issued to students will have "ISSUED TO STUDENT" stamped prominently across each page.

When copied the word COPY appears prominently across the face of the entire document. Bleach will turn the paper brown if the transcript is official. Further documentation may be obtained by contacting the university.

In accordance with the Family Educational Rights and Privacy Act of 1974, as amended, this transcript is released to you on the condition that it will not be made available to any other party without the written consent of the student.

Evolution of the AACRAO
Academic Record and Transcript Guide

Ⓐ Ⓑ Ⓒ Ⓓ Ⓔ Ⓕ

The American Association of Collegiate Registrars and Admissions Officers has long been concerned with the integrity, ease of interpretation, and technological and privacy aspects of transmission of transcripts.

This *Guide* is only one of numerous resources—both publications and workshops—developed by AACRAO to assist its members. The list of "Additional Resources," following the Glossary, highlights the pertinent ones.

The Association was founded in 1910. At the second Annual Meeting, held in Boston in 1911, a committee was appointed to "give further consideration to the problem of devising a uniform blank for the transfer of a student's record."

While initial efforts were focused upon the development of a uniform transcript blank for most, if not all, colleges and universities, the aim since 1942 has been to agree on essential items of information which should be included. Those essential items were listed in the 1945 *Guide* and in the 1947 reprint. The 1949 *Supplement*, reissued in 1950, added brief explanations or definitions for each item.

The revision of 1952 included discussions of transcript evaluation, forged transcripts, transcripts for teacher licensing needs, and a bibliography.

The 1959 *Guide* reflected advances in transcript design made in cooperation with the National Association of State Directors of Teacher Education and Certification.

It also abstracted a report entitled "The Recording and Reporting of Student Disciplinary Records"—a report that was developed jointly with and adopted by AACRAO, the American College Personnel Association, the National Association of Women Deans and Counselors, and the National Association of Student Personnel Administrators. Recommendations of the Association of Graduate Deans were also considered as to the arrangement of essential items.

In 1965, the *Guide* included a formal resolution of the State Directors of Teacher Education and Certification concerning the acceptance of a transcript as a document to facilitate teacher certification. The *Guide* also incorporated the recommendations of the Committee on Improvement of Student Personnel Records of the Council of Graduate Schools of the United States, and addressed the use of "reproducing equipment" for transcripts. In addition, the 1965 edition included modifications of essential transcript items, with explanations, and contained as an appendix "A Guide to Good Practices in the Recording and Reporting of Student Disciplinary Records"—a guide which was replaced by the 1970 AACRAO statement entitled *Release of Information About Students: A Guide.*

The *Guide* was thoroughly revised in 1971.

The 1977 *Guide* reflected the changes brought about by the passage of the Family Educational Rights and Privacy Act of 1974, as amended, and also contained information and recommendations on continuing education and nontraditional education records.

The 1984 *Guide* differentiated between the content of academic records, the content of academic transcripts, and the content of other institutional records. The 1984 edition also responded to an increased need for security awareness by including, as an appendix, a self-audit of record and transcript policies and practices. Another appendix provided sample transcript forms to aid colleges and universities planning for revision of basic records systems and transcript production.

The 1996 AACRAO Academic Record and Transcript Guide built on previous work, and also addressed new issues. It built on the distinction between academic records and academic transcripts by listing all components according to their suitability to appear on the transcript, or only in the database. It evaluated each component for suitability for transcript and/or database on a scale that we continue in the 2003 edition: Essential, Recommended, Optional, or Not Recommended. The

1996 edition identified "disciplinary action" as an item that should be maintained by the institution in its database, but which should not appear on the academic transcript. Reflecting a new interest in the electronic exchange of data, the 1996 *Guide* added such a chapter. Other new features in the 1996 edition included an expanded section on nontraditional courses, a sample transcript key, and a suggested reading list.

The 2003 *Guide*:

- Updates the discussion of Database and Transcript Components;
- Provides an updated "Key to the Transcript;"
- Addresses three current issues as previewed in the introductory chapter, along with an Appendix which summarizes two AACRAO surveys on those subjects;
- Briefly summarizes the current impact of FERPA and the USA PATRIOT Act on the release of student educational records;

- Expands the discussion of "Transcript Services: Issuing, Withholding, and Faxing;"
- Updates the discussion of:
  - ▶ Fraudulent Transcripts—along with an Appendix containing "Guidelines for Fighting Fraud;"
  - ▶ Security of Records;
  - ▶ Continuing Education Unit (CEU) Records;

- Expands and updates, with examples in another Appendix, the discussion of the transcription of nontraditional learning; and
- Clarifies the two standards—one current (EDI) and one emerging (XML)—for "Electronic Standards for Data Interchange."

A thoroughly revised Glossary, a greatly expanded list of "Additional Resources," and an Index complete *The AACRAO 2003 Academic Record and Transcript Guide*.

Glossary

Academic Dismissal or Suspension: An individual's involuntary separation from the institution for failure to maintain academic standards. Academic suspension differs from academic dismissal in that academic suspension implies or states conditions under which readmission will be permitted, while academic dismissal is final.

Academic Forgiveness or Bankruptcy: A policy allowing certain portions of a student's prior educational history to be removed from the computation of the student's cumulative credit and grade point average totals. A typical policy includes the removal of all or a portion of the prior academic record from the cumulative totals after a specified period of non-attendance at that or other institutions. Most policies on academic forgiveness or bankruptcy require the student to request this process. Many institutions have a "repeat policy" that allows the first or all prior attempts of the same course to be excluded from the cumulative totals and cumulative grade point average. It is important that the history be removed only from the cumulative totals; no courses or grades should be deleted from the academic record or transcript.

Academic Probation or Warning: Denotes that a student's academic performance is below the standard defined by the institution.

Academic Record: A document or electronic image maintained by the office of the registrar that reflects the unabridged academic history of the student at the institution. It contains a chronological listing of the student's total quantitative and qualitative learning experiences and may include any information pertinent to the evaluation.

ACT Code: A code assigned to colleges and universities in the United States and Canada by the American College Testing Program.

ANSI or the American National Standards Institute: An organization that promulgates voluntary standards that have become accepted across a wide variety of industries. One of its many committees is the Accredited Standards Committee x12, which sets national standards for the exchange of electronic data. See Chapter Twelve, "Electronic Standards for Data Interchange."

Calendar System: Defines the type of academic session (*e.g.,* semester, quarter, trimester, etc.).

CEEB Code: A code assigned to colleges and universities in the United States and Canada by the Educational Testing Service and authorized by the College Entrance Examination Board, commonly known as The College Board.

CIP or Classification of Instructional Programs: A coding structure administered by the U.S. Department of Education, National Center for Education Statistics to classify academic programs by content.

Class Rank: The position of a student in an academic grouping.

Continuing Education Unit (CEU): Ten contact hours of participation in an organized continuing education experience under responsible sponsorship, capable direction, and qualified instruction. These educational experiences are used to maintain certification in many professional fields. However, CEUs should not be considered analogous to academic course work, and are not included in the academic transcript. See Chapter Ten, "Continuing Education

Unit Records," for a listing of data elements which should be recorded on the CEU transcript.

Course Identification: Typically includes the discipline or department abbreviation, course number, descriptive title, and number of credits associated with the course. The specific descriptive title should be the same as the one used in that year's catalog. If abbreviations are used, care should be taken to make them intelligible.

Credit: The unit used to represent courses quantitatively. The number of credits assigned to a course is usually determined by the number of in-class hours per week, exclusive of laboratory periods, and the number of weeks in the session. One credit is usually assigned to a class that meets 50 minutes a week over a period of a quarter, semester, or term.

Credit Conversion: Credit conversion from quarter-hour credits to semester-hour credits is accomplished by multiplying the number of quarter-hour credits by ⅔; to convert from semester-hour credits to quarter-hour credits, multiply the number of semester hour credits by ⅓.

Database: In the broadest sense includes all data collected and maintained by the institution in any medium. More commonly, it refers to those items of data, often stored as coded values, that are maintained in the institutional computerized database.

Dates of Attendance: The starting and ending dates of a term, a course within the term, or a session. Actual dates (month, day and year) should be indicated on the transcript, if possible. If not possible, approximate dates may be designated by the academic year, i.e., Fall or First (or 1) Semester or year. When designating terms as first, second, etc., start with the fall term. For special terms, courses, or sessions that do not fit the traditional calendars, it is even more important that the exact beginning and ending dates (day, month, year) be indicated.

Where nontraditional learning is involved, see Chapter Nine for calendar considerations.

Degree Audit: An internal advising document that typically includes both degree and program requirements and an extract of the academic history of the student. A typical degree audit program matches the requirements for the student's degree and program with the courses that the student has completed and is currently taking. A degree audit frequently includes additional information such as the student's academic status, test scores, proficiencies completed, etc.

Demonstrated Competencies: Nonclassroom experiences for which credit is awarded. Examples include military experience, life experience, CLEP, AP, PEP, other nationally standardized examinations, and institutional examinations.

Demonstrated Proficiencies: Typically degree or program requirements such as English or mathematics proficiency, foreign language proficiency, public service, etc. that have been completed by the student. The institution maintains records of these proficiencies in the institutional database, but since credit usually is not awarded, notations of proficiencies are not included on the transcript.

Distance Learning: Consists of courses that take place free of time or space limitations, in whole or in part; such courses may be offered entirely or partly in ways that are web-based, web-enhanced, delivered through interactive video, or via other technologies.

Electronic Standards for Data Interchange: The electronic exchange of student data is currently occurring via two standards. One is EDI (Electronic Data Interchange); the other is XML (Extensible Markup Language). EDI standards have been approved by the American National Standards Institute (ANSI) for various transactions, including the exchange of transcripts. XML is an emerging standard. See

XML, in the Glossary; see generally Chapter Twelve, "Electronic Standards for Data Interchange: EDI and XML," for more details.

Electronic Portfolio: A student-created compilation of accomplishments and interests, stored digitally on a computer hard drive or in removable media (floppy disk, zip disk, CD, etc.). Generally sent by the student, rather than by the registrar's office.

Eligible to Continue or Re-enroll: A status that indicates the student may continue enrollment or may re-enroll at the institution without any special action required on the part of the student or institution. See "Recording Academic and Disciplinary Action on Transcripts" in Chapter Five.

Family Educational Rights and Privacy Act of 1974, as amended (FERPA): An act of Congress that defines the parameters of access to student educational records. Institutional policies and procedures governing release of information about students must be based upon the provisions of the Act. See Chapter Six, "FERPA, USA PATRIOT Act, and Their Impact on Release of Student Education Records."

FERPA Re-disclosure Statement: A statement recommended to be included on the transcript to comply with FERPA requirements. A sample statement would be: "In accordance with the Family Educational Rights and Privacy Act of 1974, as amended, this record is released to you on the condition that it will not be made available to any other party without the written consent of the student." See Chapter Four, "Key to the Transcript," required items; and see generally, Chapter Six, on FERPA.

FICE (Federal Interagency Commission on Education) Code: Administered and maintained by the U.S. Department of Education's National Center for Education Statistics, it is used to identify institutions of higher education in the United States.

Good Standing: Status often denotes that the student is not on probation and/or is eligible to continue enrollment or re-enroll.

Grade: A qualitative rating or evaluation of a student's achievement, and is most frequently expressed on a letter scale. Grades of A, B, C, D generally correspond to the terms "excellent," "good," "satisfactory," and "lowest passing quality." The grade of E or F represents "failure" and is unacceptable for credit in a course. Some institutions use a plus or minus to further delineate a letter grade. Other grading systems sometimes used are Pass/Fail, Pass/No Record, Satisfactory/Unsatisfactory, and Credit/No Credit.

Grade Points: Numerical values assigned to letter grades to provide a basis for calculating grade point averages; the most common scheme is the 4-point system: A=4, B=3, C=2, D=1, E or F=0.

Grade Point Average (GPA): An arithmetic ratio denoting the overall quality of a student's academic record. The GPA is commonly calculated by 1) multiplying the credits for each course by the grade points associated with the grade earned, 2) totaling the points earned for all courses, and 3) dividing the total points by the total number of graded credits attempted, as defined by the institution.

Graduation Statement: Identifies on the transcript degrees awarded by the issuing institution, including dates, majors, and honors, if applicable.

Key to the Transcript: Provides information that is needed by the recipient of the transcript to interpret the record properly. It is recommended that the key be printed on the back of the transcript, but it may be a separate document that accompanies each transcript issued.

Last Entry Notation: A message or series of symbols signifying that no further entries should follow on a student's transcript.

[95]

Location and Identification of the Institution: Includes the street address, city, state, zip code, and country, if applicable. If may also include other helpful identifying information such as telephone and fax numbers; e-mail address; office URL; FICE, CEEB and ACT codes.

Major: A prescribed number of courses, usually representing between a fourth and a third of the total required for the degree, in an academic discipline. Completion of the major is designed to assure disciplined and cumulative study, carried on over an extended period of time, in an important field of intellectual inquiry.

Major Area of Study: Denotes the specialty within an academic discipline in which the student is enrolled, *e.g.*, "social psychology" within "psychology." Similar terms sometimes used are "concentration" or "emphasis."

Minor Area of Study: A prescribed number of courses, usually about half of the number required for the major, in an academic discipline. Completion of the minor is designed to assure more than an introduction to an important intellectual field of inquiry.

Name Changes: See "Name of Student" below.

Name of the Institution: An institution's corporate or legal name. In complex institutions, the names of separate administrative units and their locations may be different from that of the main campus.

Name of Student: Includes family name and all given names. Nicknames may be included in the institutional database, but should not be used on the transcript. For other permutations, see "Name Change Recommendation" in Chapter Five.

Narrative Evaluation: A written assessment of the quality and characteristics of student performance and achievement. The narrative may stand alone, or supplement the conventional evaluation information.

Nontraditional Learning: Varies from traditional classroom work either in its method of delivery (see "Distance Learning" definition) or in its origin outside the classroom (military, experiential, corporate, etc.) For examples of such learning and suggestions as to how such nontraditional educational experiences can be transcripted, see Chapter Nine, "Transcription of Nontraditional Work" and Appendix C, "Examples of Nontraditional Transcript Entries."

Official Transcript: Normally a transcript that has been received directly from the issuing institution. A paper official transcript should include the college seal or its facsimile, date of issue, and an appropriate signature or facsimile.

Prior Postsecondary Education: Includes names and locations of all colleges and universities previously attended, with periods of attendance, degrees earned, and transfer credits accepted.

Quarter: A term during which classes are normally in session for ten weeks. An institution on the quarter system usually has three quarters (fall, winter, spring) in the academic year; a fourth quarter may be offered as a summer term.

Secondary School Graduation: Denotes the date of graduation and name and location of the secondary school from which the individual received a diploma.

Semester: A term in which classes are normally in session for fifteen weeks. In a semester system, there are normally two semesters (fall and spring) in an academic year.

SPEEDE/ExPress: A special task force, appointed in 1988 by the AACRAO Executive Committee, to explore the feasibility of creating a national standard format to exchange student transcripts directly from one educational institution to another using electronic media. That task force is now the AACRAO Committee on Standardization of Postsecondary Education Electronic Data Exchange (SPEEDE). The Pre-Kindergarten through Grade 12 task force became the task force on the Exchange of Permanent Records Electronically for Students and Schools (ExPRESS). The combined standards are now known as the SPEEDE/ExPRESS formats. See Chapter Twelve, "Electronic Standards for Data Interchange," for a fuller discussion.

Student Identification Number: Any unique number assigned to the student by the institution. (See Chapter Five for a discussion of use of Social Security Number as student identification.)

Term: A specific period of the year during which classes are in session. See Quarter, Semester.

Transcript: A document created from the academic record that is used to review the academic performance of the student.

Trimester: One segment of an academic year, when that year includes three semesters. See Semester.

Type of Credit: Type of Credit should be clearly labeled if credit is awarded on the basis of nonclassroom experiences such as military or life experience, qualifying scores on national or local examinations, or corporate education. See Appendix C, "Examples of Nontraditional Transcript Entries."

USA PATRIOT Act ("Uniting and Strengthening America by Providing Appropriate Tools Required to Intercept and Obstruct Terrorism") (October 25, 2001): Passed after the attacks of September 11, 2001, the Act allows institutions of higher education to provide—without student consent—education records related to a terrorism investigation, upon presentation of a court order from an Assistant U.S. Attorney General or higher official, certifying that "specific and articulable facts" support the request. See Chapter Six, "FERPA, USA PATRIOT Act, and Their Impact on Release of Student Education Records."

XML (Extensible Markup Language): An emerging standard for the electronic transmission of student education records. AACRAO's SPEEDE Committee and the Postsecondary Electronic Standards Council (PESC) are working with the American National Standards Institute (ANSI) to get the XML standard for sending and receiving transcripts approved by Committee X12 of ANSI. See Chapter Twelve, "Electronic Standards for Data Interchange: EDI and XML."

[97]

References and Resources

References

Mallet, C. E. 1924. *A History of the University of Oxford, London.* London: Methuen.

National Association of College and University Attorneys (NACUA). 1995. *The Permissibility of Withholding Transcripts Under the Bankruptcy Law* (2nd ed.) Washington, D.C.

Quann, C. James. 1994. Changing the Nom de Plume—A Name-Changing Protocol. *College and University.* Winter 69(2): 76–82.

Quann, C. James and Associates. 1979. *Admissions, Academic Records and Registrar Services: A Handbook of Policies and Procedures.* San Francisco: Jossey Bass Publishers.

Additional Resources

American Association of Collegiate Registrars and Admissions Officers

The AACRAO Web site, periodicals, and publications are all sources of practical guidance and information. Here is a selection of resources of most interest to registrars:

AACRAO WEB SITE (WWW.AACRAO.ORG)

■ *"Compliance" Section*—Ongoing updates on FERPA, SEVIS, IPEDS, and other regulations affecting records and reporting.

> NOTE Expanded FERPA content can be found on the AACRAO Web site, including: the *FERPA Guide Online*; a presentation on "Training Faculty and Staff on FERPA;" and a "FERPA Exam." Related material covering the Solomon Amendment, Student Right-to-Know Act, etc. is also available.

■ *"Resource Center"*—is a depository for papers and presentations that have been contributed by AACRAO members and other individuals in the profession. Topics range from Academic Calendars to Wireless Technology. Also contains information on FERPA under "Records and Registration."

AACRAO PERIODICALS

■ *College and University (C&U)*—The Association's research journal; focuses on emerging concerns and new techniques; also contains book reviews and practical tips.

■ *SEM Monthly*—Focuses on Strategic Enrollment Management, with additional reports on developments in law, technology, and international admissions.

■ *Transcript*—Transmitted through electronic mail, AACRAO's weekly electronic newsletter features a wide variety of articles pertinent to admissions, registration, and current trends in higher education.

■ *AACRAO Update*—A newsletter that covers AACRAO and interassociation news.

AACRAO PUBLICATIONS

The AACRAO Web site, under "Publications," lists all publications currently available from AACRAO. These are particularly pertinent to registrars:

Academic Calendar—
■ *2000–2001 Academic Calendars Study: Analytical Profiles of Calendar Use and Conversions.* Downloadable for AACRAO members at the "Publications" section of the Web site. Contains references to websites of institutions implementing or considering calendar conversions.

FERPA-related—
■ *The AACRAO 2001 FERPA Guide* (Richard A. Rainsberger, chair; Eliott G. Baker, Dennis Hicks, Brad Myers, Jim Noe, and Faith A. Weese). A reference for personnel in higher education containing 7 chapters and 16 appendices, featuring "How Would You Handle...?" (a chapter with solutions

to numerous scenarios), the full text of FERPA, and several sample compliance documents.

■ *FERPA and Secondary Education: The Family Educational Rights and Privacy Act of 1974 as amended and the Student* (Richard A. Rainsberger, 1997). A reference for K-12 school officials.

■ *FERPA Guide Online.* Online tutorial, on AACRAO Web site (under "Publications.")

Fraudulent Academic Credentials—
■ *Bogus U.S. Institutions: How to Avoid Fake Schools and Fake Degrees.* (1988). Provides information on accrediting bodies and tips on uncovering diploma mills.

■ *Misrepresentation in the Marketplace and Beyond: Ethics Under Siege.* (1996).

Privacy-related—
■ *AACRAO Fax Guidelines*—Free; prepared by the AACRAO Fax Guideline Task Force (Dennis J. Dulniak, Chair; Janet L. Busekist; Carol J. Cline; Mary K. Jones; and Keith M. White.) (1996). Downloadable at www.aacrao.com/about/ faxguide.html.

■ *Final Report NSF [National Science Foundation]— LAMP [Logging and Monitoring Privacy] Project: Identifying Where Technology Logging and Monitoring for Increased Security End and Violations of Personal Privacy and Student Records Begin.* Virginia E. Rezmierski and Nathaniel St. Clair. AACRAO, 2001. Discusses logging activities and when such activities require limitations, guidelines, and additional training of personnel; also discusses log data in relation to FERPA.

■ *Privacy and the Handling of Student Information in the Electronic Networked Environments of Colleges and Universities.* A white paper developed by a CAUSE task force in cooperation with AACRAO. Recommends principles for fair information practice. Contains many examples of actual events involving technology and privacy. Among its eight appendices is a "Checklist for Privacy Policy and Fair Information Practices."

Records Management—
■ *Student Records Management: A Handbook.* Edited by M. Therese Ruzicka and Beth Lee Weckmueller. Order through Greenwood Publishing Group, 88 Post Road West, P.O. Box 5007, Westport, CT 06881-5007; phone (203) 226-3571; fax (203) 222-1502.

Retention of Records—
■ *AACRAO's Retention of Records: Guide for Retention and Disposal of Student Records.* (2000). Includes Retention Schedule A (For Applicants Who Do Not Enroll, Whether Accepted or Rejected), and Retention Schedule B (Admissions Data/Documents for Applicants Who Enroll). Also includes Appendix D, "Policies Covering Disposition of Academic Records of Closed Schools."

Self-Audit—
■ *AACRAO's Professional Development Guidelines for Registrars: A Self-Audit* (2000). Featured sections include: "Electronic Communication;" "Transcript Processes and Procedures;" "Information Technology and Support Equipment;" and "Legal Issues" (FERPA; Solomon Amendment; and Student Right-to-Know Act). See AACRAO's Web site (www.aacrao.org) for ongoing updates.

For a complete listing of AACRAO publications, visit www.aacrao.org/publications/catalog.

AACRAO PROFESSIONAL DEVELOPMENT

AACRAO offers highly focused seminars and workshops to help keep you current with the latest in enrollment management, records and registration, information technology, and student services. Check AACRAO's Web site for the latest offerings at www.aacrao.org/meetings.

American Council on Education (ACE)

ACE WEB SITE (WWW.ACENET.EDU)

■ *Memorandum on Anti-Terrorism Legislation.* Legal memorandum on the USA PATRIOT Act. First section discusses impact on the registrar and the international student office. Available at www.acenet.edu/washington/anti_terror/2001/2001_anti_terror.pdf.

ALL LISTED ON THE ACE WEB SITE AT WWW.ACENET.EDU/CALEC/CORPORATE

■ *Guide to the Evaluation of Educational Experiences in the Armed Forces.* Between publication dates, ACE provides a supplement entitled *Handbook to the Guide to the Evaluation of Educational Experiences in the Armed Services.*

■ *Guide to Educational Credit by Examination.*

■ *National Guide to Educational Credit for Training Programs.*

CENTER FOR ADULT LEARNING
(A DIVISION OF ACE)

Maintains a service for recording Continuing Education Units (CEUs) on a national basis. See www.acenet.edu/calec/corporate/ceu.cfm.

On CEUs, see also The International Association for Continuing Education and Training at www.iacet.org/about/about.htm

"FindLaw"

■ An excellent public resource for finding laws, regulations, and caselaw at the state and federal level, and internationally. See www.findlaw.com.

National Association of College and University Attorneys (NACUA)

■ *The Family Educational Rights and Privacy Act: A General Overview.*
■ *The Family Educational Rights and Privacy Act: A Legal Compendium.*

NOTE Neither is downloadable online, but both can be ordered at www.nacua.org

National Association of College and University Business Officers (NACUBO)

■ *Campus Crime Reporting: A Guide to Clery Act Compliance.* See www.nacubo.org. (Publication is not downloadable online but can be ordered from NACUBO.)

Postsecondary Electronic Standards Council (PESC)

■ *A Guide to the Implementation of Electronic Transcripts and Student Records, Version 4.0.* Postsecondary Electronic Standards Council: Washington, DC, April 1998. Available at www.standardscouncil.org.

"Thomas"

■ A source on U.S. Federal legislation. It is put out by the Library of Congress, and contains bill summaries, committee information, and links to the Congressional Record. See thomas.loc.gov.

U.S. Department of Education (USDE)

■ *Family Policy Compliance Office*—This is the office of the USDE that is responsible for enforcing/administering the Family Educational Rights and Privacy Act of 1974, as amended. The FPCO has responsibility for FERPA at all levels of education (K–12 and postsecondary). See www.ed.gov/offices/OM/fpco.

[101]

Index

[104]